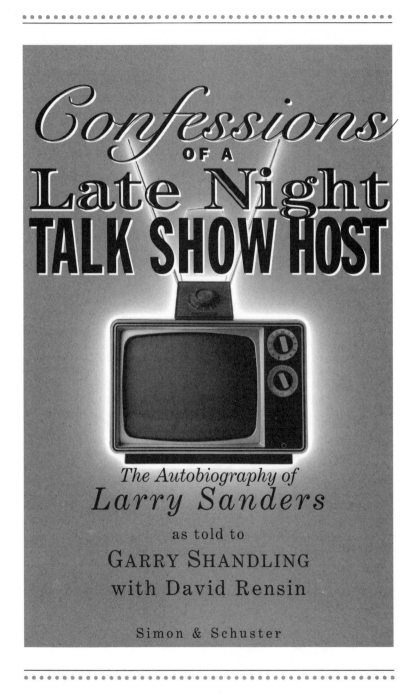

Confessions
OF A
Late Night
TALK SHOW HOST

The Autobiography of
Larry Sanders

as told to

GARRY SHANDLING
with David Rensin

Simon & Schuster

SIMON & SCHUSTER
Rockefeller Center
1230 Avenue of the Americas
New York, NY 10020

Design and interior production by Robert Bull Design

Manufactured in the United States of America

10 9 8 7 6 5 4 3 2 1

Library of Congress Cataloging-in-Publication Data is available.

ISBN 0-684-81204-5

Photographs on pages 136, 140, 144–145, 146–147, 148–149, 150–151, 152–153,
154–155, 170, 171, 172–173, 174–175, 176–177, 182–183, 191, 194–195, 198,
200–201, 204, 205, 208–209, and 210–211 by Bernard Fallon, © Home Box Office,
A Division of Time Warner Entertainment Company, L.P.

Photographs on pages 134–135, 137, 138–139, 141, 142–143, 156–157, 158–159,
160–161, 162–163, 164–165, 166–167, 168–169, 178–179, 180–181, 184–185,
186–187, 188–189, 190, 192–193, 196, 197, 199, 202–203, 206–207, 212, 213,
214–215, and 216 by Larry Watson, © Home Box Office, A Division of Time
Warner Entertainment Company, L.P.

Photograph of television set copyright © 1998 Photodisc Inc.

To me

PART ONE

INTRO-
DUCTION

Why Now?

WHY AM I WRITING THIS AUTOBIO-
graphy now?

Because I'm Larry Sanders.

I'm famous.

Actually, I'm very, very, very famous,
but the publisher said that title wouldn't
fit on the cover of the book. Who
wouldn't be famous if they hosted a late
night network talk show opposite David
Letterman and Jay Leno, and, before
them, opposite Johnny Carson? I've
been in the talk show game now for
fifteen years, and while Arsenio
Hall, Chevy Chase, Dick Cavett,
Joan Rivers, Magic John-
son, Merv

Griffin, Mike Douglas, Alan Thicke, Pat Sajak, and even Johnny Carson have all had what they think were successful runs, I outlasted them all. I was on the air until just six months ago.

It seems like only yesterday that I said good-bye to all of you on my finale, mainly because I've had only one good night's sleep since. I toss and turn for hours until I realize that making salad isn't going to relax me. I have been flooded with letters that scream, "Larry, we miss you!" "Larry, don't leave us!" "Mr. Sanders, we need more of you!" Okay, that was just one letter, but I am sure the post office lost millions more that contain the exact same message, and there are probably another five to ten million fans who wrote similar letters but were embarrassed to mail them or couldn't afford the postage. That would be a total of close to twelve million letters. Perhaps I *had* left too soon. I never considered that my television audience was so codependent, so unable to function without me—in other words, so sexy. It is with a deep sense of compassion and caring about others and with no ego whatsoever that I come back to you just like Jesus did, to speak to you one last time about something even more riveting than that of which Jesus spoke: show business and all the gossip and dirt and rumors that I have accumulated over a lifetime. And two thousand years from now, after translation upon translation of my book, who knows how I will finally be perceived? Maybe I'll be thought of as the real Son of God.

To answer the question I am asked most, "What makes you a television star and not me?" My response: "Huge psychological dysfunction." I am driven to be loved by everyone. Only the Olsen twins want it more. On television, you can be loved by millions of people; in fact, there is an expression, "making love to the camera," which refers to the idea of seducing the audience right through the lens, and the actor ultimately making love to them and then packing up and going home. I want to put your mind at ease by telling you that for the last ten years I have been making love to you through the camera every night, and on all but two of those nights, I wore a condom. Those two nights I was drunk and forgot. Sorry.

The first time I ever considered telling my life story was a few years ago, when Roseanne appeared on my show to promote her book *My Lives*. I'd spent five minutes reading it cover to cover in the makeup chair before airtime, and when I put it down I said to our makeup man, "Well, this isn't *that* good. I could do better than this. My life is more interesting than all of her lives put together. Dammit, my nose is still shining. Do something, you bastard!"

"Then maybe you can get a couple of bucks for it at the used bookstore, you asshole," said Roseanne, sliding into the makeup chair next to me. She'd lost so much weight since her last appearance that I hadn't noticed her come in. I quickly dropped her book in my lap and picked up Rush Limbaugh's. *He's* fat. And so was his book. Both of them need to lose about twenty pages.

"You can't fool me, Larry," she said, "I know you are talking about my book. I see it in your lap."

"Oh, this?" I said, fumbling for it. "I'm sure it's wonderful. Do I need to read it before we talk? Or should I just let you run with it? I absolutely trust your instincts."

"I'll take care of it," she said. "Like always."

"That's why we love to have you on the show, Rosie," I said, as I stood and left the room.

By the way, the show went wonderfully. Rosie never mentioned the makeup room incident or, for that matter, the book, and I took one of her personalities—Darla the hooker, I think—out for dinner afterward.

But that night, after I paid for sex, I couldn't sleep. Something was bothering me. Then I realized what it was. The interview had not gone that well, and the show was weak. I love Roseanne, and I hope her new talk show is successful no matter who hosts it.

Days later, I went to my psychologist, who shall remain nameless, and I said, "Dr. Reisman, here's my problem. I read Roseanne's book, and . . ." Dr. Reisman interrupted me and said, "I have that book on tape, but I'm a slow listener and haven't gotten through it yet."

"Why are Geraldo and Howard Stern and Roseanne and Burt Reynolds and Tina Turner and Richard Pryor and Louie Anderson and Brett Butler being asked to write books?" I asked. "Granted, I have no severe diseases, and my career hasn't started to go really downhill yet, but no one has asked me to write even a pamphlet."

"Well, is that something you really have the time to do?" he asked. "Is that something you really *want* to do?"

I said, "No, but that's not the issue. The issue is why haven't they asked me." At which point Dr. Reisman said, "You've got me thinking: No one's ever asked *me* to write a book, either." He seemed oddly disturbed. That's when I realized that Dr. Reisman should be seeing a shrink himself. Why would anyone ask him to write a book? He's not on TV or radio or the movies. His therapy might pass for comedy, but it was full of dated material that you could hear at any Friars Club roast. Most of his jokes were stolen from Pat Morita and Freud's father, who was hilarious. But Dr. Reisman got so upset at the thought of not being a sought-after author that I had to waste two precious minutes of *my* session talking him down. I was fine with that, but when he took two of my Xanax and borrowed a couple Valium for later, I got angry and said, "You've crossed the line, pal; that's *my* illegal medication."

Finally, I said, "Can we get back to me and my concerns about writing my best-selling book?"

He said, "You, like every celebrity who writes a story about their life, will find it exhilaratingly self-indulgent. Write it for yourself and read it for yourself."

I wanted one more very important opinion before committing to this book, so I asked my producer, Artie. Over the years, I've come to depend on Artie. There's something priceless and extremely annoying about someone who will always tell you the truth, or at least lie to you in a way that, although you know it's a lie, sounds a lot like the truth. In the end, you know that person has your best interests at heart because, after all, he or she depends on you for a paycheck.

"It's your ass, kiddo," Artie said, in his no-nonsense manner. "If it were me, I wouldn't do it. But that's just me."

"Really? Why wouldn't you do it?" I asked.

"Simple. I'd have to tell the truth, and I can't," he said.

"What do you mean you'd have to tell the truth, and you can't?" I asked. "I thought you always told me the truth."

"Of course I do. That's my job."

"Oh. I feel better now," I said.

"Look, Larry," Artie explained. "You'll be opening up a can of worms because you have to continue to have guests on the show and booking is difficult enough. If you're going to tell stories about people who have been on the show, they may not want to come back again. We might not be able to book anybody except the lady who makes presidents' faces out of potato chips, unless you somehow manage to insult her, too."

"I would never do that," I said. "Although remember how mad that bitch got when she caught Hank eating Eisenhower?"

Artie continued, "Plus, you will take the chance of alienating your coworkers—any number of the crew who I've seen drunk during the production of the show."

"Come on, Artie," I protested. "I would never write that about you."

"I'm not telling you what to do," Artie said. "I've got enough on my mind without having to get involved with you and Hank and your goddamned books."

"Hank's writing a book, too?" Hank, by the way, is my sidekick on the show. He's Ed McMahon to my Johnny Carson, Regis Philbin to my Joey Bishop, Clarabell to my Buffalo Bob.

"Yes," Artie said. "It's called *The Sidekick's Book*. Don't worry. There's not that many sidekicks who will buy it. McMahon's retired, Regis has his own show, and Andy Richter would just shoplift it."

"But, you know, I think Hank's book could do really well in the relationship/self-help market," I said. "In every relationship, there is a star and there is a sidekick . . . Sometimes it's called husband and wife."

"Speak for yourself," said Artie.

"I am," I said, as I looked around to see if anyone else was there.

Artie was on his way out the door when I thought of one more question. "Did Hank say how big his advance was?"

"Come on, Larry. It's *Hank*," Artie said.

My heart sank. "Shit, that's what I was afraid of," I

said. "Between the fan clubs and the right wing of the Republican Party, he'll probably clean up."

"Right. But remember, homosexuals, liberals, dancers, acrobats, and mimes make up a big part of the world too, Larry. Just don't say I didn't warn you," Artie said as he walked away.

Artie knew me too well. I felt like I wanted to run down the hall like a little girl, jump on my bed, and pound the pillows until my fists were blue. Even so, I felt that I had to do what I had to do and write my book. I authorized my new agent, Stevie Grant, to call publishing companies to see why none had approached me to write my story and to see if anyone would be interested in *Confessions of a Late Night Talk Show Host: The Autobiography of Larry Sanders*. That wasn't the original title I'd come up with, but it's the one that Hank said would guarantee me getting the book into Kmart. Just so you know, the other titles were: *See Me, Feel Me, Read Me; I Cry as Hard as I Laugh; My Weight;* and *Far from an Asshole*.

I can't say that it surprised me that every publisher was interested. They said, "Gosh, we wished we had known that you wanted to write a book about a man struggling to balance the artificial show business life with something more meaningful—whatever that is. We would have come to you first."

I think they assumed that I was just a one-dimensional talk show host who simply sat in his chair and could only

talk to the people on his right. In fact, I'm a deep man who can talk to people on either side.

Stevie Grant immediately got offers for the story of how I clawed my way to the top. I turned them down. The money was just too little. I didn't think the effort to write would be worth the trouble. Then the offers came in higher, then so high that I realized, philosophically, that it would be unfair of me not to go ahead and write the book and do something good for myself. It would be unfair to turn down the money because I could use it to add on to my house, which is something that brings me true happiness. This summer I'm installing a follow-spot in my master bedroom.

For a long time I'd wanted to build a new office in my house as well. I had run out of room, frankly, to store all my awards and plaques. It had gotten so bad that I nearly lost a Golden Globe in the Northridge earthquake, when one of them—the only one—fell off a crowded shelf and hurtled toward the floor. I tried to grab it as it fell but I wasn't fast enough. Thank God it hit my dog, so it didn't get marred. Savage, my black lab, was only out for a second. When he woke up I yelled, "Good boy!" and gave him a biscuit. I've never seen him look more confused.

There's No Law Against Gossip

A BOOK LIKE THIS HAS TO INCLUDE some gossip or it won't sell. At least that's what I was told by the publishers. While some think gossip is a sin—and I'm one of them, and so is Tony Danza, but please don't say you heard it from me—it's not against the law. Sure, if we passed such a law the world would be a better place, but who has the strength to take on that responsibility? Gossip hurts everyone. By becoming absorbed in someone else's life, we lose focus on our own. And the person who is being gossiped about may, in fact, be an innocent who suffers intense humiliation. I know. Remember in 1991 when everyone thought I put a gerbil up my ass? Totally false. I'm uncomfortable even putting one in my shirt pocket, let alone my ass.

I wish a law could be passed that would prevent sensationalistic books like this one, which exploit others for entertainment value, from ever being published again. I hope that this will be the last book of that type. The new law should start right after this book is published. This book would then become quite a collector's item and triple in value. Maybe as you sit there on the toilet you are holding in both your hands quite a valuable investment—and, of course, I'm assuming it's this book.

So enjoy.

PART TWO

YOUNG LARRY

My Early Years

I WAS A FAT CHILD. I COULDN'T get girls in high school. I couldn't even get guys. My dad drank. My mom drank. My dog drank. Basically, I got no love. In second grade the kids called me "four eyes" even though I didn't wear glasses. In fifth grade, when I did start wearing glasses, they called me "six eyes."

I was never elected to any office in high school, although I was impeached three times. Each time my parents were called to school, they chose to go to Europe instead. I was rejected by everyone except for a very nice old man who gave me candy through the school fence and flashed me. Something even my father wouldn't do—he'd flash me, but there was no candy.

Unbeknownst to most everyone except those of you who regularly read those trashy tabloids—and that would be all of you—I have suffered through many personal tragedies: an unhappy and abusive childhood, two divorces, many empty love affairs, a venereal disease that nearly took my right leg, feuds, substance dependencies, a palimony suit from my mother, who said, "You live with me twenty years and you move out just like that? This will cost you," and worst of all, the horror of being rear-ended backstage by one of Siegfried and Roy's big white leopards. There was a rumor that those cats in their act were gay because they were far more theatrical than cats in the wild, and someone reported seeing one of them blowing the other one in the fountain at Caesar's. Siegfried insisted they were just "cleaning" each other.

My parents met on a street corner in Minneapolis in the winter of 1946. While waiting to cross, Mom had slipped and fallen on the ice, and Dad stepped on her and kept walking. Another man quickly helped my mother up. He said to my dad, "Don't you think you owe this woman an apology?" And my dad said, "It's not my fault she's clumsy and fell on the ice in such a way that someone in a rush like me wouldn't see her there."

"Well, she could sue you," said the stranger.

"I'm very sorry, ma'am," my dad said quickly to her. "I wish I hadn't stepped on you. I sincerely apologize.

That man standing next to me tripped you and shoved you down and then pushed me on top of you. May I help you across the street?"

When they got to the other side, Dad still wasn't convinced that Mom wasn't going to sue, so he asked her out on a date and ultimately married her for the same reason. In fact, the vows included the words "and not sue you until death do us part." They discovered they were both welders during the war, though my mom lost her job when the fighting men returned home, and she was forced to sell cosmetics at Woolworth's, although she so missed her old occupation she still wore the welder's helmet.

I was born in 1950. Although my parents shredded my birth certificate, burned it, and scattered the ashes over the Pacific, I pieced it back together after an intensive eighteen-year search with the help of noted DNA expert Barry Scheck—who told me he could get anyone convicted or acquitted, depending on which side he represented.

My parents and I lived in a tract house in Mound, a suburb of Minneapolis. My father made my mother quit her job at Woolworth's to stay home and take care of me. By then, my mother had grown tired of being pushed around and stepped on by men, and whatever romantic flame my parents once had simply burned out, so that there was a lot of coldness in the house. Only after I'd grown up did I realize that my parents kept the thermostat at a constant sixty-two degrees, no matter what the season. Needless to say, they did not raise me with much emotion, much touching, or much love. I'm sure that has *something* to do with the reason that I'm reaching out for the love of an audience—and a heater.

Dad was a small man, but on the job he did the work of two small men. Then, every night at 6:30, he would come home to our two-bedroom frame house with the aluminum siding that he'd put up himself, have a beer, and ask my mother what was for dinner. At the table, Dad would always kid around and say the food tasted like shit. Dad was very witty, and that was one of his good ones.

After dinner, Dad would turn on the TV. He rarely watched it, just turned it on to drown out my mother in case she tried to bring up the subject of the possible lawsuit again. Then he'd maybe pick up a newspaper or a book or clean his blowtorch. If I had done nothing wrong that day, there would be no spanking—or torching, as the case may be. If I was lucky, he would only beat me.

Torching is an unusual form of child abuse. I don't think there are any support groups for victims, even today. I'm just starting to accept it. I suppose it could have been worse. I could have been sexually abused, like I've read in so many revealing celebrity autobiographies. But after I was born, my parents were hardly interested in having sex with each other, let alone me, so I consider myself lucky. I had to wait until my first marriage to experience sexual abuse, and then there was plenty of it. And most of it was directed toward me.

I Thought
I Was Special

BECAUSE I WAS BORN ON DECEMBER 31, I got to stay up and watch the fireworks at midnight. I always thought they were for me because that's what my parents told me. I remember exploding colors filled the night sky during one of the few times, as a child, I felt blessed and special. Only when I turned fifteen did I discover that the fireworks were a New Year's Eve tradition that had absolutely nothing to do with my birthday. My parents had lied to me. I was even more upset to discover that the ball in Times Square fell completely oblivious to me and my own balls, which also drop at midnight.

I found that out the night I was at a party with some high school friends. I was waiting patiently for the gang to remember to sing "Happy Birthday." It was almost midnight, and I was beginning to think they had forgotten. That's when the crowd suddenly grew excited and people started cheering. A very pretty girl came up to kiss me.

"Happy New Year," she said.

"Thank you," I said, after we kissed. Her lips tasted strangely salty. "And by the way, it's okay that you didn't get me anything."

"What are you talking about?" she said.

"Well, you know, not everybody has to feel they have to give me a present on my birthday."

"When *is* your birthday?"

That's when I started to get dizzy, realizing she didn't know. I said, "It's today, don't you know that? That's why the country is having this big celebration."

She said, "You're funny." I wasn't trying to be funny, but I've always remembered that moment because it was the first time anyone said that to me. Otherwise, I was devastated and nauseous. I wasn't as special as I had been led to believe.

"One day," I swore, "I'm going to be special again. And get my balls fixed."

My Repressed
Sex Life

LIKE MANY KIDS, I LEARNED ABOUT
sex from movies and television. I thought
sex magazines were cheap and sleazy, especially the good ones.

I first learned about the mysteries of
love—and by that I mean I had my first
orgasm—when I was thirteen. I have
heard that women can have multiple
orgasms, but I'll believe it when I see it. I
should say now that every time I have
sex with a different woman, it's as
though it's my first time. In fact,
each time I have sex with the same
woman it is like the first time,

because the previous ones would never really hold up in court.

Maybe it was fate playing an ironic joke, but Johnny Carson helped initiate me into the adolescent world that would be my home for almost thirty years. It was 1963. I was lying face down on the couch, watching *The Tonight Show*. Shelley Berman was on, perched on the edge of his stool, waiting for his prop phone to ring, and I was thinking, "Boy, that routine is so predictable I don't know why anyone bothers to laugh anymore." I also thought, "Boy, that's what I want to do some day." After Shelley Berman, Johnny introduced Raquel Welch. She walked onto the set, and I just came on the couch. Another thing to blame on the dog. Since it was my first orgasm, I didn't know quite what had happened. I felt good, but I was scared because I thought I was bleeding.

Ironically, when I was thirty-seven, I was sitting in my office at *The Larry Sanders Show* when Artie stuck his head in the door and said, "Raquel Welch's person called." That's always been a wonderful show business phrase, "person," meaning her agent—which is such a lie, because an agent is not really a person. It's one of the many paradoxes in show business. I had never told Artie the story of my sexual awakening because it was none of his damn business, and I knew it would eventually make a good story for a book and I didn't want anyone to steal it, like Dennis Miller or someone. So I concealed my excitement and stayed cool. "Well, I would love to have her on," I said, even though what I meant was, "I surely would love to have another orgasm in my pants."

I was nervous the whole day waiting for Raquel to arrive. I wondered, "Am I going to tell her? Am I not going to tell her? Will I be attracted to her when I see her? Wouldn't it be something if her reaction to me was the same as mine was to her because, after all, now I'm on TV, too?" I assume that of all the millions out there, someone must have an orgasm when I walk through the curtains. I know I do.

By three o'clock, when the guests arrived, I could hardly contain myself. I knew she was supposed to show up any minute. The whole day I kept asking Paula, our talent booker, "By the way, is Raquel Welch fucking here yet?" I tossed it off in a way that kept her from reading through my anxiety. Finally, I figured I'd just get up and walk down the hallway and around by the dressing rooms. I hadn't gone ten feet when suddenly the elevator doors parted, and just like that scene in *Close Encounters* when the spaceship opens and bright light floods out, there was this magical moment. It was Raquel Welch. I started to walk toward her . . . and then fell to my knees because I had the most powerful orgasm of the day. Everyone thought I was having a stroke. "Get your hands off me," I yelled, "I'm fine. I just slipped on the ice."

Ninety minutes later, the monologue was over and I was sitting at my desk. I picked up my note cards and held them, nervously, until the band stopped playing. Then I said, "And now our first guest, a fine actress and a woman who needs no introduction: Raquel Welch."

She came out through the curtains, and I instinctively held on to my chair. Every sexual urge I had had when I was thirteen shot through me again. I couldn't even stand to greet her. She is one of the only women ever on the show for whom I didn't stand up and give a little hug or show business kiss. Then she came over and sat on the couch and I said, "Forgive me for not standing. I twisted my knee earlier."

"How's your stroke?" she asked. We were off to a great interview.

Raquel's spot went so well that she has returned to the show many times. We've never slept together—because I wouldn't want to have to talk to her afterward—but she *is* a very sexy and talented woman who, I understand, has slept with much of the crew, including Sid, the cue card man. That was shocking to me but, evidently, Sid is hung like a cameraman. I would marry Raquel Welch tomorrow. None of today's sex symbols can hold a candle to her except for David Duchovny.

My Mother, the
Easy Stage Mother

I WAS IN COLLEGE WHEN I DISCOVERED that my mother, Karen, slept around quite a lot. I think she slept with everyone, or so everyone has told me. One day I bumped into Jerry Lewis backstage at the Muscular Dystrophy Telethon. He winked at me in a way that suggested that he, too, had been with my mother. He also had that year's poster boy on his lap, and he was trying to teach him Dean Martin's straight lines and delivery. He'd gotten the poor kid drunk, and the kid was so happy they thought for a moment alcohol was the cure.

Jerry Lewis is a comedic

genius and an incredibly giving man with relentless energy when it comes to helping others. I greatly admire him. Evidently, so did my mother.

My mom was, in show business parlance, a stage mother. When I was a child, Mom was always going to Vegas. First with me and Dad, then with her girlfriends, and eventually alone. But when she wasn't pushing pennies into the slots, she'd hang around outside stage doors looking for action. She was well known to security guards up and down the Strip for trying to sleep with performers like Tony Bennett, Tom Jones, Rich Little, and the Righteous Brothers. The Barosini chimps also seemed to recognize her when she was in the audience.

I'm also sure Redd Foxx, may he rest in peace, fucked my mother. I realized this one day when I was listening to a Redd Foxx album in college. Redd was right in the middle of his famous "getting the pussy stuck in the front door" routine. My mother, who was visiting, started to sob.

"What is *so* sad?" I asked, concerned.

"I'm sorry. I'm sorry. That story's about me!" she blurted out.

"What?"

"Remember when you were a little boy and your daddy and I took you to Las Vegas and we went to see Redd Foxx?"

"No."

"Maybe it wasn't your daddy, but Redd Foxx made a

move on me. I was flattered, but I said no. But this was at a time when your dad and I were a little shaky. So, I called Redd the next day and I went up to his hotel room and we had sex. He called all his friends: Ike Turner, Frank Sinatra, Shirley MacLaine, Sammy. There were others. I don't remember them all. All I can tell you is everyone left the room happy except me and Sammy. He'd had a bad show the night before, and there was just nothing I could do."

I put my hand on her shoulder and said, "Mom, why are you telling me this now?"

"I know," she whimpered. "I know. I should be telling this to your little brother."

"What little brother? I'm an only child."

"No," she said. "Tito Jackson is your little brother. Remember when I went away for the summer? We told you I was going to the fat farm to lose weight. Now you know. You are related to Tito Jackson."

I couldn't hide my disappointment. "Gee, Mom," I said, "you've slept with more men than Paul Lynde."

"Don't make fun of Paul Lynde. I slept with him, too."

By the way, I've had Tito Jackson on the show many times, but the subject of our mother has never come up.

Good-bye Virginity, Hello Hollywood

IF RAQUEL WELCH HELPED ACQUAINT me with the fruit of my loins through TV, then Edna, a waitress at Denny's, was the first real woman who showed me how to plant the seeds. I was fifteen. She was forty-two and Scandinavian. It was perfect. If she had been any younger or from America I would have said, "No thanks." But a foreigner old enough to be my mother: "Va va va vooom." My friends and I used to hang out at Denny's after school, and she would sneak us coffee even though she knew it wasn't healthy for young men to drink.

Whenever Edna served the gang, she would brush against me. What's odd is that she actually used a brush to do it. I believe it was the same brush she used to clean the crumbs off the table. For weeks, then months, I thought it was really just because there was something on my shirt or pants that needed to be swept away. I didn't realize she was coming on to me until one day when she said, "Would you like to have sex with me?"

Then she said, "I need to move a lot of books out of my living room. Would you mind coming to help me on Saturday afternoon?" I noticed she was stirring my coffee with a condom. So I went over to her apartment to help. I knocked on the door and she said, "Larry, is that you?" I said, "Maybe." She opened the door and stood there completely naked. The first thing I noticed was that she didn't have her brush. I said, "Where's your brush?" and she said, "It's in here," and walked me into her bedroom.

She had lied to me. There was no brush. There was just her, spread-eagled on the bed with runway strobe lights lined up to guide my approach in case, I guess, it was foggy. I don't remember my first time being something that encouraged me to have sex a second time, mainly because I overshot the bed and made a water landing in her tub. Emergency crews from several adjacent states rushed in. The panicked scene prevented me from attempting sex with Edna again until she was seventy-two, when the sex was so good she choked and died.

Back at home, the emotional and physical abuse got worse as I got older.

When I was eighteen, my dad constructed a discipline closet. From the outside, it looked like a sauna and it was practically soundproof. That way, when we had guests, no one knew anybody was inside or that anything was wrong. If guests brought their loofahs and towels, Dad would just say the sauna was broken. To this day, whenever I do stand-up in Minneapolis and see kids I went to school with, they tease me by asking if my lazy father ever got the sauna fixed. I have to say no and keep to myself the horrible secret, that Dad would make me go in there. "You're sentenced to eight hours in solitary, you little Jew," he'd say. Life was difficult because I was the only Jewish kid in my family.

It was very dark inside the so-called sauna. I knew my father was on the other side of the door because I could hear the television. My dad would just sit there for hours watching it. I thought, "Maybe if I were on TV, Dad would listen to and watch me." That's when I knew it was time to come out of the closet. I had a calling and was ready to openly speak of it and accept it. If he didn't love me for who I was, so be it. I had found myself. I could feel it in most of my bones: I wanted to be a talk show host! When I announced it to my father, he sobbed uncontrollably. "I'd rather you be a homosexual than *this*." I could never please him. I knew deep down that if I had told him I was gay, he would have beaten the shit out of me and cried even harder. There was no winning.

I sold my old Camaro and bought a pink van that I packed to the gills with hopes and dreams and headed for Hollywood to prove that I could be a talk show host and straight . The van ran out of gas five miles out of town, not a good sign. But a sign.

PART
THREE

CHASING
THE
RAINBOW

Joan Embery

BEFORE HEADING TO LOS ANGELES I stopped in San Diego to visit a college friend. We went to the San Diego Zoo, and I remember that at one point we were looking down into the zebra pit and arguing about whether they had white stripes on black or black stripes on white. We were having the same argument about the acid. I knew my friend was particularly stoned because he was looking through a pay telescope for twenty minutes before realizing he had to put a dime in it.

Suddenly a young woman walked out of the zebra stalls. She could not have been more than twenty-two. She wore safari shorts and a khaki top, exactly the same outfit I had on. I yelled at her, "Hey, nice clothes!" She looked up—because that's not something a visitor would yell at the zebras—and she saw a mirror image of herself as a young, good-looking guy. She smiled.

I yelled, "My name's Larry. Larry Sanders."

"My name's Joan. Joan Embery," she yelled back.

I walked a little closer and said, "What are you doing after the zebras?" The next thing I know, she invited me to help her feed the coyotes. We talked and flirted while she showed me how the animals lived.

Eventually we exhausted the small talk and she asked me, "What do you do?"

I said, "I'm a comedian and I'm going to Los Angeles because I hope to become a major talk show host."

"Are you going to try that right away," she asked, "or will you do a game show first, like Johnny Carson?" I hadn't decided, but even so, I remember being quite excited that she didn't act as if my dreams were queer or self-centered.

"I have a vision," I said, "and that vision is sitting behind the host's desk, talking to Bert Convy." (May he rest in peace. I wish, today, that I'd never bumped him off the show. He died before we got a chance to reschedule. But I did have sex in his hot tub once. It was about a month after he'd passed away and I'd gone over to his house to pay my respects to his family.)

Joan confessed that her dream was simply "to work with the animals."

I said, "You have quite a personality and you're very beautiful. You should consider doing some television work yourself. Maybe one day, when I'm a talk show host, I'll get to interview you and you'll bring some animals on my show." She started to say something, but before she could finish I kissed her. She smelled of raw meat, hay, and Charlie, my favorite perfume. The combination was intoxicating. When we stopped kissing I said, "I'm sorry I interrupted you," and she said, "It's okay. I was just going to say that you'd stepped in a little coyote stool." Then she grabbed my hand and led me into the coyote cave, where they all have private suites and a grotto like Hef has at the Playboy Mansion. "They also have parties here after the zoo closes, but you can't tell anyone," Joan said, as she started undressing. She removed her knapsack and twirled it around like she was Gypsy Rose Lee.

We had sex right there in the coyote cave at the San Diego Zoo. What I'll always remember is that just as I was reaching my climax, I noticed that there were two coyotes just sitting there in awe, thinking they had never seen anyone have sex in the missionary position.

Later, when we said our good-byes, she smiled that smile that made the animals trust her and said, "Hey, I'm going to think about what you said about doing some television." She shoved an animal treat in my mouth and patted my head.

Years later, even before I had my own show, I saw her on *The Tonight Show* with Johnny Carson. She'd brought on a small monkey and it peed on Johnny's shoulder. It didn't surprise me or make me jealous. I'd always known that Joan could do it. That night I was proud she'd taken my advice. Finally, when I got my own talk show, she came on. I wasn't even sure if she would remember our very private history, until she brought out the first animals. They were coyotes.

She said, "These are twenty-one-year-old coyotes from the zoo." She smiled at me. The coyotes both licked my hand. I swear to God, they recognized me.

I haven't seen Joan since then. We preferred having on Jack Hanna from the Cleveland Zoo. He has a fresher approach.

The Comedy Store

I LEFT SAN DIEGO WITH A WARM GLOW, and arrived in Hollywood three hours later. It was 1979 or 1992. I wish my memory was better. The sun had set and it was dark; I didn't know my way around, and I had no place to go.

I figured I might as well get a head start on making my dream of becoming a major talk show host come true. I'd been working on my comedy routine in the car during the drive from Minneapolis, but even though the material was excellent, I needed more than just one person laughing and clapping. So I decided to find somewhere I could try it out. I drove down Sunset Boulevard until I hit the Strip. A hooker standing in front of the Sunset Hyatt House Hotel motioned to me. We were discussing prices when I noticed a sign on a building to the west. It read,

THE COMEDY STORE.

Luck was with me. It was amateur night.

I signed in.

Amateur night at the Comedy Store is a very humiliating experience because you have to sign a list with fifty or sixty other hopeful young comedians and comediennes, and then just wait for Mitzi Shore, the owner of the Comedy Store, to announce your name. You sit and wait and pray that they call your name and that you'll get five minutes on stage. I signed in around seven P.M. By nine P.M., I was completely drunk. I'd have a little sip here, a little sip there. I noticed people were getting angry, so I bought my own drink. It was about ten o'clock when someone came up to me and said, "Are you Larry Sanders?" I said, "Yes." He said, "Mitzi says you're next." Even though I was already drunk, I was in the habit of needing a drink before I went onstage, so I went to the bar and had another one.

Then Mitzi Shore called my name. Of course, nobody knew me. It was, "Who's Larry Sanders? Some kid just off the bus from Minnesota." That's how they announced me: "Who's Larry Sanders? Some kid just off the bus from Minnesota." That hurt my feelings.

My first routine was very different from my act now. I opened with, "I'm from Minneapolis, but I like to come to L.A. for the summers." That got a laugh, but nothing from the other 250 people who were there. I followed with, "When I was in high school, the vice principal committed suicide by sneaking into the gymnasium one day and hanging himself on the rings in the gym. The next day, our physical education coach found him dead, hanging in the rings, and gave him a 9.8." That got two laughs. The athletic theme was working, so I said, "We had a guy on our gymnastics team who used to smoke a lot of pot. One day, they caught him trying to feed a carrot to the side horse." This one hit pay dirt. Everyone in the place booed. I decided to go for it all and said, "I had a stupid English teacher who got a sundial and then got a hernia trying to wind it." It was one huge laugh after another until I listened later to the tape recording I had made, which revealed that I had bombed miserably.

I needed work. I've heard there are only a couple of comics who were naturals their first time up: Cosby and Louie Anderson—who was also from Minneapolis. Some people would put Gallagher in that group, but I saw Gallagher when he started out, and he was so nervous that when he tried to hit a watermelon with his sledgehammer, he'd miss and hit some poor jerk in the front row instead. Not as funny. There was lots of blood. It took him years to get it right.

I walked off the Comedy Store stage to ringing

applause. People were thrilled that I was done. I had another drink and decided to stick around awhile to watch the competition.

I didn't know it at the time, but there were two other young comics in the room that night waiting to go on. Both of them would one day become my best friends.

The first was a young man of Spanish extraction with a mustache. He went on after me and, frankly, what he did I wouldn't do to my dog, or my mother. As part of my old act—the act I did that night—I would occasionally look at a beautiful woman in the audience to say, "You're looking good." And I had another whole routine I used to do about "It's not my job."

When this guy took the stage almost the first things out of his mouth were "Looking good!" and "It's not my job!" The only differences were the Chicano accent and the exclamation point.

I hadn't realized that comedians stole other comedians' material! Just a little while later that truth would be driven home again. Another joke I did involved saying "dynamite" over and over again, and I could hardly believe what I was hearing when a gawky young black guy got up on stage and he started saying, "dy-no-mite!" Worse, he had stretched out the word and milked the pronunciation far beyond what I had ever thought possible.

I felt betrayed. It's a feeling I've experienced often in my career, and yet, even though it's often written off as a common occupational hazard in this business, I've never been willing to accept it—like so many of my friends. And former friends, who claim I stole material from them, which I would never do intentionally.

I turned to the guy standing next to me at the back of the Big Room. He looked funny and had prematurely gray hair, a wide and silly smile, and an arrow through his head. He, too, was waiting to go on. Another loser, I thought. I said, "Excuse me . . ." He didn't answer. I repeated myself. "Excuse me." Still, no answer. "I said, exxcuu-useeee me!" He turned.

"Who is that?" I asked, pointing to the lanky black guy on stage, who had stolen my material.

"Jimmie Walker," he said.

"Well, he's stolen part of my act," I said. "I'm the one who says 'dynamite' and I'm the one who has that little run about white people. And that Mexican guy who was on about an hour ago. He also stole from me."

My new friend tried to reassure me. "What are you, just off the bus? Everybody steals from everybody. Don't worry about it."

To my surprise, Mitzi Shore invited me to come back anytime. As I was about to leave the club and look for a motel, the two guys who had each stolen part of my act came bounding up. I couldn't believe their nerve. The Mexican guy—actually he looked Jewish and a little like Geraldo Rivera—said, "Hey, we think you've got something. You're really looking good." His name, of course, was Freddie Prinze. Then, he introduced me to his friend.

"Your stuff is dy-no-mite!" said the black guy, "or my name isn't . . ."

". . . Jimmie Walker," I said, forcing a smile. Since they liked me, we quickly became inseparable.

Gabe Kaplan was also at the Comedy Store my first evening there. He did a set in the Belly Room and then just hung out and bragged to the other comics about the big house he'd recently bought. Before that, it turned out, he'd lived in the same apartment building as Freddie and Jimmie.

When the club closed, Freddie suggested that we all go up and see Gabe's new place, but for some reason Gabe didn't want any of the guys coming over. Jimmie started kidding Gabe about "suddenly being too good for his old friends," but Gabe apologized and said he was just a loner who was too good for his old friends.

I later went to Gabe's house many times. Usually we'd sit in front of his television and make insulting remarks about comics we knew while watching their sit-coms or routines on *The Tonight Show*. And every few weekends Gabe would host a wild party that sometimes lasted for days. I never saw either Freddie or Jimmie there. Gabe wasn't a loner after all, just too good for his old friends. I couldn't wait to be like that.

Besides my own memorable debut, what I remember most about that night at the Comedy Store was Gabe standing in the spotlight onstage. I realized that I had never in my life, being from Minnesota, seen anyone who looked so Jewish. I thought, "My goodness, the audience is probably going to hate him." You discover as you travel through this country performing that much of America really shies away from Jews, and this was a guy who was getting right up in front of people and was clearly Jewish. I learned later that he had gotten a nose job to try and hide the fact, but he had that kinky hair and there was no disguising it. Often, when he would go onstage, if he started to do well one of the comics in the back of the room would actually shout out, "He's a Jew!" and watch Gabe battle that for the next ten minutes. Once the audience knows you're a Jew, it's an uphill fight. Ask Clint Eastwood, who denies being Jewish to this day, as does Michelle Pfeiffer, who *really does* look Jewish.

By the end of the evening—it was already morning, really—at one of Gabe's parties I asked him if there were any apartments for rent in the building. One of the hookers said, "I believe 4G is available." The place was tiny, but I was so used to being in a closet most of my life that I was able to get very comfortable. Of course, the apartment was so small that it had no closet, so I had to hang all of my clothes above my head, over the bed, and I felt even more at home.

Years later, when Freddie Prinze was doing so well with *Chico and the Man,* he moved up to a four-room penthouse in our building. As you know, Freddie killed himself soon after. It was a terrible tragedy and his apartment became available, so I took it.

Moonlighting

WHEN YOU'RE JUST STARTING OUT, stand-up comedy doesn't pay the bills. So I took a job waiting tables at Joe Allen's restaurant. It was, at the time, a well-known industry hangout in Beverly Hills. I thought I might meet some important people who would want to help out a funny waiter. But I was always working the tables on the patio. That's outdoors. The laughs go right up into the air. You can't hear anything. It's a bad, bad room. All the waiters inside were killing, getting big laughs. I was bombing every night only because I was outdoors. Every time

I would try to deliver a joke to some industry hotshot, a car horn would honk or a bird would squawk or a gunshot would ring out.

I quit Joe Allen's after a month. I knew I could do better than that. My next job was writing jokes for Rodney Dangerfield. But we went our separate ways over creative differences when I tried to convince Rodney to change "I get no respect" to "I get no pussy."

"You can still pull your tie when you say the line," I said. "Plus, yanking the Windsor knot will now be metaphorically correct."

But Rodney refused to listen. "Hey, I'm the comedian here," he said. "Stop pulling your own schwantz and gimme some respect if you want to keep your job."

"Fine, I get the picture," I said.

I began writing for Joan Rivers. We had the exact same confrontation. I tried to convince her to change "Can we talk?" to "Can we fuck?" "Edgier," I told her, "plus, less Jewish."

I was fired again. Clearly, I marched to a different drummer, even though I had no musical ability whatsoever.

Joan Rivers is a wonderful, sweet woman, and I wear her jewelry all the time when I have someplace sad to go.

I Didn't Always Work Alone

COMEDY BECAME MY LIFE. I WORKED the road, going from city to city, club to club, brick wall to brick wall. Many women wanted to sleep with me after the show. Some even wanted to have sex. It was easy to get used to the idea. After all, I'm a sharing person. I've shared myself gladly with my fans. I've shared myself intimately with two wives. I shared myself with my dog, may she rest in peace. But the person with whom I shared the most important part —my career—was a man named Stan Paxton.

Stan Paxton was my

stand-up partner in the seventies or eighties. I really have a bad memory. I'm only positive it wasn't in the forties.

We met in college. We were both class clowns who ended up in the same class, shouting out jokes at the same time. The difference between Stan and me is that I'm funny. Stan is also self-destructive. Even at the University of Minnesota, he was a heavy, heavy drinker and a big gambler. And he didn't have the money to support either of his vices, so he was constantly broke and begging me for money. Then I would have to go onstage and attempt to be funny with this guy who I felt was a real loser and was holding me back. I'm sure I felt much the same way Tommy Smothers felt about his brother Mike, whom he had to replace with his sister Dick.

In college, Stan and I used to appear at student functions and play local nightclubs. The incident that most clearly expresses our dynamic was the time Stan and I drove to St. Paul to do a show. We took Stan's Mustang. Or what I thought was Stan's Mustang. It turned out to be a stolen car that Stan had swapped for his saxophone and $500. He'd also stolen the saxophone and the $500. Stan always put himself and others in jeopardy. Fortunately he had a gift of gab, which for a long time kept him out of serious trouble, except onstage where he would lock up and faint.

Finally, I said, "I've got to get away from you. You're holding me back." I had forgotten we were onstage. The audience was aghast. Stan blushed. I tried to turn it into something funny. "You're a fucking loser!" I yelled. "You drink. You steal cars. You speed. And you've got three grams of coke in your pocket. You're lucky if you won't be dead in a year." I tried to build on it even further: "I hate you and everyone like you." The act never came together.

I thought I'd seen the last of Stan until one night, a few months later, I was coming off the stage at the Comedy Store, and there, standing in front of me, was Stan Paxton, a drink in his hand and cocaine smeared all over his face.

"Sanders, you asshole," said Stan, "how's it hanging?"

"Stan," I said, "you're wearing your blow a little heavy. You look like a mime."

I bought Stan a few drinks and we sat at the bar and talked over old times. He seemed to be enjoying himself, which he always did when he did most of the talking. I wasn't really paying attention. I was just waiting to find out what he was doing in Los Angeles, in the Comedy Store, on a night I just happened to be performing. I knew he wanted something.

Finally it came out. Stan told me, "I want to get the act back together again." It didn't surprise me. It would have surprised me if he hadn't asked. "It will be just like old times," he said.

"That's what I'm afraid of," I said. "What's the problem? Do you owe those people money again?" "Those people" was our old code for the Mob. But Stan wasn't listening.

"We're like the next Martin and Lewis," he said.

"Right," I said. "Even though neither one of us sings."

"More like the next Smothers Brothers?" Stan asked.

"No, because we're not related," I said. So we had a huge argument at the bar over whose place we were next in line to take. The argument threw into sharp focus the conceptual problems we'd had from the start. We just had different sensibilities. We couldn't even get the comparisons right. As it turned out, we were closest to the next Tammy Faye and Jim Bakker, because one day we would split apart completely and one of us would wind up in jail and the other would wear his makeup too heavily. But I always give in—a trait I wish more of the women I dated had.

Stan and I were together again. This time the partnership lasted a couple of years, although a couple shows would have been just as okay with me. We worked at all the Los Angeles comedy clubs, did some TV, and went on the road together.

Stan was there when I met Francine, the woman who would become my first wife. In fact, Stan was always there when I met any girl during those years. He would always try to horn in on any available woman I was talking to. When I couldn't find Stan, I would look behind my date. Nine times out of ten he would be there. Sometimes as I was kissing a woman I would reach around her with my hand only to find Stan, trying to get his nose up her ass.

"This couldn't have been how Nichols and May started," I thought.

Stan and I got the opportunity to make a comedy

album called *I'm Larry, He's Stan.* Today it's a classic. In fact, there's only one in existence. We arrived at that title after much fighting. He wanted to call it *I'm Stan, He's Larry,* but I said I wouldn't do it unless it was *I'm Larry, He's Stan.* One good reason was that when we would walk onstage, I would speak first to the audience and say, "I'm Larry, he's Stan."

"If we changed the names around, what would I say?" I asked Stan. "I can't walk out and say, 'He's Larry, I'm Stan.'" I wasn't going to settle for talking to the audience second. You can see how these creative problems just snowballed into an unimaginably complicated situation. Sort of like Wayland Flowers and Madame, may they rest in peace. Stan's final pitch was *I'm Stan, He's Not Stan.* I was so mad that I nearly killed us both. "Hey, jump off this cliff with me," I asked nicely.

We finally settled the title dispute because I just insisted. I said, "*I'm Larry, He's Stan* sounds more intelligent and is, in fact, funnier." Stan bought the argument because he's an idiot. I said that if he wasn't happy with *I'm Larry, He's Stan,* that I'd be perfectly happy with *I'm Larry and I Don't Know Who This Other Guy Is.* These were dark days made even darker at night.

I remember when the Smothers Brothers caught our act at the Swedish Dinner Theater in the Valley. Tom Smothers, who's a hero of mine, came up to me and said, right to my face, "I thought you were hilarious and I wish you the best of luck. I think you're going to be really successful, Stan." I said, "No, I'm Larry." It crushed me that he had gotten my name wrong. It crushed me that Tom didn't even know which one I was. *"He's* Stan, Tom," I said.

"I'm Dick," he replied. Tom is the funny one who plays the guitar and acts silly, right? Or is that Dick? Anyway, one of them really insulted me.

Lots of people told me to get rid of Stan. They said he was a liability to my career. Jerry Stiller and Anne Meara both told me to dump him. So did Rowan and Martin. So did two young comediennes who would one day, years later, become "The Mommies." Even Willie Tyler and Lester told me to ax Stan.

Willie Tyler is a wonderful black ventriloquist. Lester is his black dummy. I've never seen a white comedian with a black dummy. That would be racist. Although I wouldn't mind seeing a Jew working a Nazi. To be honest, it was Lester who came up to me and said, "Get rid of your partner. Or put your hand up his ass and start working his mouth."

Then Willie said, "Is that a nice thing to say, Lester?"

"Did I say that, or did you?" said Lester.

"Well, I can see your lips moving, Lester, so it must have been you."

I can't watch a ventriloquist because I'm uncomfortable seeing a man sitting on another man's knee, even if one of them isn't real.

My First Marriage

AS I SAID, STAN WAS THERE WHEN I met the other partner in my life. Francine was my first wife. If only I could have loved her as much as I loved the audience. Or maybe if there could have been two hundred of her. Even when I have sex with one woman, I refer to it as "standing room only."

I met Francine in 1978, when Stan and I did a weekend at the Cleveland Comedy Club. She was in the audience. She had a date. In one part of the act I would ask the audience whether there was anybody living together, but not married. She raised her hand and then I said, "That's sort of like leasing with an option to buy, isn't it?"

After everyone stopped laughing I said to her, "How long have you been living together?"

She said a year and a half.

I said to her date, "Isn't it about time to shit or get off the pot?" Before he could answer, I said to the audience, "Isn't that a romantic way of phrasing it? There's a romantic term, 'shit or get off the pot.' It's like, okay, I better get married, honey, because I've got to take a big dump."

Then I looked right at Francine and said, "If you're not married after living together a year and a half, then he's not marrying you." Then I looked right at her date and said, "Are you going to marry her? Why don't you just tell her the wedding date right now?" He laughed awkwardly. I kept pushing.

After the show I wanted to see Francine, to apologize to her date and to make a move on her. She and I made some small talk, and I could tell that she was attracted to me because she was talking deeply into my mouth. So I just came right out and said, "I'm staying at the Redwood Inn," which was a $14-a-night, seedy hotel where I stayed when I worked in Cleveland, but they charged $200 a night. Onstage I always mention the hotel I stay at so that any woman who is interested in finding me, can. I never mention the room number, though, because I don't want to seem desperate. By the way, I was on the road so much that my penis has a tag on it that says, "Drop in any mail-box; we guarantee postage."

Francine showed up a half hour after the show at my door. "What you said was right. I shouldn't be just living with someone for a year and a half. There's something wrong. I must be codependent. Why do I pick men who can't commit? Maybe because my father abandoned me . . ." I found myself losing interest in having sex with her, but she kept talking anyway. She told me she worked on the assembly line at Ford. "Putting cars together—especially the seats—makes me feel special." I found the simplicity of her desires in life very endearing. If only she could have expressed them more quickly.

Just then Stan showed up with a couple of hookers. I had to pay them off, as usual. Typically, Stan didn't even think to share them with me, but these two were particularly unattractive. Nothing happened that night, and the next day I left for Akron and another gig.

Two weeks later, after I'd returned to Los Angeles, I was very lonely one night and I called up Francine. By the end of the conversation, without realizing it, I'd agreed to send her the airline fare to come and visit me. She arrived the following weekend on a super-saver ticket. She brought so much luggage that it seemed as though she'd packed everything she owned, and had come not to visit, but to move in. She opened one suitcase and all of her dishes and a torchiere lamp fell out. I knew I was in trouble.

She didn't say anything about moving in and neither

did I, although I dropped the phrase "moving out" a few times. It was great to have her in my apartment, and the lamp fit perfectly in the corner. During the next few days I showed her all over Los Angeles. We had a really nice time. She seemed very normal, in that Midwestern way. Show business didn't impress her, nor did I. And she never went back to Cleveland.

Fast-forward two-and-a-half years. Francine and I had moved into Freddie Prinze's old penthouse apartment. One day she said to me, "Do you remember when we met and you said, 'If you live with someone longer than a year and a half, there's something wrong'?"

I said, "Of course I remember that!"

"And that a woman should have more self-esteem? Well, we've been living together two-and-a-half years now," she said.

She had me. It was a quick civil ceremony with Stan as the only witness, though I'm not sure he actually saw anything because most of the time he was in a chair in the corner, puking on a bridesmaid.

Marriage can be wonderful. But for me it was also distracting. Being in show business requires that a person really focus totally on their career. You can't really afford, when you're starting out, to care much about anyone else. That's also true later, when you're successful, but for a different reason: If you care about someone, they just end up hurting you and taking half your money.

Even though Francine and I were husband and wife, I knew in my heart that she could really only be an accessory to my career. I think Francine finally caught on to me when I introduced us to another couple by saying, "Hi. I'm Larry, she's Stan." I was, in a hyphenated word, self-centered. I had no therapist and had not read one self-help book. I was a relationship nightmare. Jason Priestley said, "You're worse than me. I at least have a sister."

For a long time I considered Francine the hottest woman who would have sex with me, until I met an actress named Kelly LeBrock. I was loitering outside the ladies' room at the Comedy Store trolling for women when we met. She gave me a glance when she went into the gals' and stopped to talk on the way out. I remember her shaking her hair in my face and saying, "You're more beautiful than me, and I hate you, but you're the only man with lips bigger than mine."

I've never worried that her then-husband, Steven Seagal, would kick my ass if he found out because we are very good friends. I don't think he'll mind if I also reveal that we once swapped wives. I took Kelly, and Steven went off with Francine. Afterward, he complained that he felt gypped and cheated. Steven said all Francine did was whine and complain and yell insulting, demeaning things like, "You call that a penis?" Or, "You call that an ass?" I said to Steven, "That's right. That's what Francine says in bed." I was relieved to hear that she had yelled it at him, too. My self-esteem shot up and I found the courage to leave her. I could do better, I thought. The very next woman I dated was a blind cocktail waitress. "You call that a penis?! You call that an ass?!" she shouted our first night in bed. I had a feeling she wasn't blind.

PART FOUR

SHOW
BUSINESS:
MY REAL
WIFE

The Tonight Show

THE GOAL OF EVERY STAND-UP COMIC is to perform on *The Tonight Show*. In Carson's day, Jim McCawley, the talent booker, had to see your act and think you were ready. Jim passed away recently, and I felt a desperate loss. He was a fan of mine and incredibly supportive. We also disliked many of the same comics, and that created a deep bond.

McCawley trolled the clubs nightly. He often had to tell someone, while remaining encouraging, that they just weren't good enough. For many the rejection was too much and they'd kill themselves on the spot. Others became network programming executives.

And then there were the chosen few whose successful careers were guaranteed by their first *Tonight Show* appearance. I was one of the lucky ones.

The first time Jim McCawley came to see Stan and me at the Comedy Store in Hollywood, Jerry Seinfeld, Steve Martin, Richard Pryor, Paul Rodriguez, Louie Anderson, and Bill Cosby were in the audience too. They'd come to watch my set, and they all made sure not to laugh when I was on. To say I was working a tough room was an understatement.

McCawley didn't stop laughing during our set. Later, he bought me a drink at the bar and said he would like to have me on *The Tonight Show*. Stan was off scoring drugs. It was my good luck, frankly, because after many years of enduring Stan's bad habits, they were finally about to pay off for me in spades.

As I said, many people told me to leave Stan. I never listened because I'm very loyal. But that night, Jim McCawley said, "I don't like the other guy." I wanted to take that to mean that he didn't like the other guy, but I wasn't sure. In showbiz there are so many subtleties and catch phrases that you have to read into what someone says. So when he said, "I don't like the other guy," I wasn't sure if he meant that or "You're not funny and I'm not interested in putting you on the show, but I don't know what else to say."

So he said, "I don't think you need this other guy."

I said, "Really? You mean Stan?"

"Yes."

What a relief!

"But you don't understand," I said. "Stan and I are old friends and we've been doing this act together for years. This will kill him. When am I on?"

That night I told Stan the truth. He then borrowed a couple hundred dollars and disappeared into the night. But I knew I owed Stan something. So I decided to go on *The Tonight Show* alone and basically do the act that Stan and I had developed. It would be my homage to Stan, whom I never would have left if I hadn't been pressured by McCawley and *The Tonight Show* because that's not my style.

It would be years before I saw Stan again, although some months later I thought I saw some bum who looked like him, only with a beard and dirty clothes, working a freeway off-ramp in the Valley. As I went by I heard him yell, "Hey, you asshole! Thanks for stealing the act!" I would have stopped but I wasn't positive it was Stan.

My Big Night

T HE NIGHT I WAS SCHEDULED TO APPEAR on *The Tonight Show*, my then-agent, Leo, drove me to the NBC studios in Burbank. Leo drove a Volkswagen Bug, which is one of the reasons I finally left him. This was at a time when most successful agents had a Mercedes or, at the very least, a Cadillac. For this reason, Leo was pretty much the laughingstock of the agent world. I have a much better agent now. He drives a new shiny black Porsche, so people know he means business.

Another reason I left Leo was that he had a horrendous habit of eating peanuts from a Styrofoam cup. He was the noisiest eater. Leo didn't close his mouth when he ate. You not only heard the crunching but also the screeching of the peanuts along the inside of the cup as he pulled them out. On top of the screeching and the crunching, he would say something stupid, usually with a mouthful of peanuts, such as, "I'm going to get you on *Star Search*." I'd say, "That's hosted by Ed McMahon. I was thinking of going on the show hosted by Johnny Carson." The peanuts would come shooting out of his mouth. "And I'm Gandhi!" he'd yell.

This is a very important part for you to know: I stuck with Leo until my new agent, Stevie Grant, came along and got me lots more money from the network to extend my contract for *The Larry Sanders Show*. I'm a very loyal man. I mean, I have very strong ethics when it comes to loyalty, and I stayed with Leo until I made it big. Everybody forgets that. That was for fifteen years. Then I hit it big and it was time for me to move on. But I stayed with Leo throughout the early years, when we were very close and he was very supportive. People forget that.

I was not cool as I waited behind the *Tonight Show* curtain for Johnny to announce me. I was very, very, very nervous. I felt like I had bad diarrhea. I know this sounds like a joke, but I had eaten at the NBC commissary, where that was the special.

I heard Johnny's voice say, "Here's a young comedian making his first appearance on our show . . . Larry Sanders."

The curtains opened, and I stepped through. I couldn't even see, the lights were so blinding. I found my mark on the floor and stood there. I shifted uncomfortably, marking time, then turned my back slightly to the audience and asked, "Is my ass too big in these pants?" They had to bleep the "ass," but the audience roared. That's when I knew everything would go smoothly. I was right. My set went great. Johnny and Ed were howling and Doc later asked for my phone number. That's when you know you really killed: when Doc asks for your phone number.

Like all young comics doing their first set on *The Tonight Show*, I hoped that Johnny would ask me over to the couch, and that we'd exchange a couple words before the commercials.

After my set, I waited while the applause seemed to go on forever. Would Johnny motion me over to the couch? I couldn't take the chance. I just started walking in that direction. Johnny intercepted me on the stage, shook my hand, leaned over, and said, "Why are you still standing here? The audience stopped applauding five minutes ago. We're in a commercial break and you're making a fool of yourself." Johnny talked to me!

I said, "Thank you, Mr. Carson. One day I hope to be a talk show host, too." He stared at me like I was a complete moron. I'd seen him give Jack Carter that look. I was flattered. I love Johnny. I owe him everything and would do anything for him. I was shocked to learn that not everyone felt the same.

The Carson Hit

THE MORE SUCCESSFUL I GOT, THE MORE successful people I met.

One was Dick Cavett.

Dick took a liking to me. I was one of the few people he knew who didn't make fun of him, and for some reason he felt he could trust me. He's also much older than I am, and I was the hot young comic on the rise. Whenever I was in New York he'd take me back to his apartment and tell me stories about himself and, say, Woody Allen, or anyone for that matter.

One night, years after the end of Cavett's run on ABC,

I was in town and we got very drunk at Dick's apartment. By the time I arrived, Dick was already pretty loose. He mentioned Johnny Carson in a heated tone and pronounced it "Connie Harson." Johnny beat Cavett consistently in the ratings. I should have been prepared for anything. But what Cavett said was so shocking that I almost still can't believe it.

He said he had a plan to have Johnny Carson bumped off. That's right. Killed. He had put a hit out on Johnny. He always used Mafioso language when he got drunk. (I, on the other hand, speak with a French accent after only one beer.) Evidently Cavett knew someone who knew someone who knew someone connected with the Mob: his mother.

At first I thought he was joking because that's the way comedians joke, about killing and so forth. But it turned out he was serious. The story is very sad and not something I like to repeat, but Dick Cavett has to be exposed for who he is: a hilarious man, a sharp wit, a potential murderer, and a good interviewer.

This, for the first time, is how the hit was supposed to go down. When Johnny was at his beach house in Malibu, he would always sun himself between noon and two on Saturday afternoons. That was a religious thing with Johnny. He would always be out on his deck. Cavett was going to have a scuba diver come out of the ocean, walk the twenty yards to Johnny's platform, grab him, sedate him, and pull him into the water. It would look like he'd drowned. And nobody would question Johnny Carson drowning in the ocean. He looks like he can't swim very well.

It was really a perfect plan because there's no need to bother with a getaway. The hit man would just swim out to sea and disappear underwater. He wouldn't have to bother trying to escape down the Pacific Coast Highway in a car, which is a chancy thing at best because the police can close off the road very quickly. It's closed almost half the year anyway, either because of mud slides or a Ben Vereen jogging accident.

Of course, we all know that Johnny Carson didn't die. This is why: Cavett was sure his plan would work and had scheduled it for June 23, 1979. But Cavett and the idiot scuba diver used the tide chart for June 23, 1978, by mistake. It was the lowest tide of the year. When the scuba diver came out of the water he realized that what normally would have been a twenty-yard walk to Johnny's deck had turned into a quarter-mile hike through rocks, shells, seaweed, garbage, and the leftover women from a party Bob Newhart had thrown the week before.

Even from that distance the diver could see Johnny and Don Rickles on Carson's deck. Also a woman who looked like a hooker, talked like a hooker, acted like a hooker, and charged for sex like a hooker. Whether she really was a hooker we'll never know. And it doesn't matter because she saved Johnny's life. She was looking out at the ocean when she suddenly screamed, "Oh God. There's a monster coming out of the ocean!"

Rickles, who was wearing a Speedo, said, "Thank you very much. Perhaps you'd also like to see my ass." Rickles has many metaphors for his penis. My favorite one is when he'll refer to it as a groundhog: "I pull it out of my pants, and if you see a shadow, that means six more weeks of winter." Johnny looked toward the ocean and saw the goofy scuba diver/hit man in tank and fins charging toward his house. Johnny immediately called his security men. Then he turned to Rickles and said, "I thought you told me you didn't give Dom DeLuise my address." Rickles waited until the diver was closer and finally yelled out, "Hey, that's my wife! Honey, haven't I asked you never to wear your nightie outside the house?"

Johnny's security men grabbed the diver. The police arrived and they arrested him. But the diver would only say he was lost—that actually he was looking for the Atlantic Ocean. Only I know that Cavett sent him to get Johnny.

Cavett is a reformed man now. I speak to him regularly and enjoy our conversations. I recently received a package from him that I've never opened. I just can't take the chance.

The Jobs Start Coming In

O NE DAY, MY THEN-AGENT LEO FINALLY came to me with what he called "big, big news."

"Larry, babe," he said, snacking on a handful of peanuts and pieces of a Styrofoam cup, "an executive from Goodson/Todman saw your act last week on *The Tonight Show* and he wants you to do a game show."

"I'm not good at game shows," I said. "Well, maybe only *The $125,000 Pyramid*, with Dick Clark. I'm very good at that one."

"They want you to *host* one of their new shows," he said.

I loved Leo's sense of humor. "A game show? I'd rather be caught getting a blow job from a hooker on the Sunset Strip than host a game show," I said, repeating the good advice my friend Hugh Grant always gave me. "I want to host a *talk* show. Isn't that what you've been trying to set up? At least a guest-hosting shot?"

"You think you're too good for it?" said Leo. "It wasn't too good for Carson."

I had a hard time getting the words out, but I finally said them. "Okay. Okay. What show? Don't tell me they're bringing back *The Match Game.* The next thing you know, they'll be bringing back *Hollywood Squares.* I want to work on a show that requires some intelligence from both the contestants and the audience," I said. "And it has to have beautiful models."

Leo said he couldn't promise anything, which I found suspicious. An agent is supposed to promise his client everything, even if he's lying. Still, I agreed to take the meeting. Then I tried to convince myself that hosting a game show might be smart after all. Because, you know, a game show is very much like a talk show in that you ask people questions, people answer them, and they get paid. There's really no difference, other than the buzzer, the prizes, and the models.

At the meeting the guy from Goodson/Todman said to me, "We're creating this game show, and we'd like you to audition for the host." I was immediately insulted. Leo hadn't said anything about an *audition*. I thought, "Who am I? Charles Nelson Reilly?" By the way, Charles is a sweet man who looks extraordinarily handsome in glasses. Unless he gets angry. His face becomes contorted and his glasses steam up on the left and ice over on the right. I don't know why. He once slapped me across my face with a sock so hard that I'm just recovering now. I have a feeling there was something in there besides his foot.

The show turned out to be the original *Family Feud*. I decided to give it a try and actually did well during a couple weeks of run-throughs. It was a good way to practice staying sharp and funny on my feet and to meet women. The families always had a cute daughter or two, and some of the moms were not bad either.

Unfortunately, they dumped me right before we went on the air, when the producers discovered that the week before I'd seduced the entire Snyder family from Grosse Pointe, Michigan. I don't know what the big deal was. They couldn't play the game very well. When asked to name the most popular items people used around the house and then threw away, one came up with "Dad."

The producers replaced me with my good friend Richard Dawson. His previous credit was as a regular on *Hogan's Heroes*. He was a wonderful entertainer who hosted *Family Feud* for nearly eight years and got great ratings before they finally had to dump the show because of low ratings. Years later, they brought back another version of *Family Feud* with Ray Combs, may he rest in peace. Ray killed himself after doing six years of that show. Who wouldn't?

With one "talk show" disappointment on my resume, I was ready to go back to doing stand-up and try to earn my shot as a guest host. But a voice in my head said words that I'd never heard before: "Kill someone on the subway. Kill someone on the subway." Fortunately, another voice I'd never heard before, a feminine voice, said, "If at first you don't succeed, try, try again." I believe that was my real voice.

Leo then arranged for me to substitute-host *The Price Is Right* when Bob Barker had to be rushed to the emergency room with a complex jaw fracture that he got when an overly enthusiastic contestant hit him with a refrigerator door. What no one knows is that he took an extra three months off to go big-game hunting in Kenya.

On my first day at work on *The Price Is Right*, I learned that what goes on backstage at a game show is the low point of human experience.

One model came up and said, "I'll have sex with you if you make sure I model in front of the more expensive gifts." I said, "Well, that's not for me to decide." She said, "Yes, it is. You can say, 'I want Janice to stand in front of the Maytag washer-dryer combination instead of Dian.'" I didn't realize those washer combinations were that expensive! What a great learning experience.

Another Big Day

"JANUARY 20, 1985. DEAR DIARY: I, Larry Sanders, guest-hosted *The Tonight Show*. I hope this leads to me getting my own talk show."

As you can see from the above diary entry, my first guest-hosting job on *The Tonight Show* was a deep, emotional experience. It was the most memorable night of my life because it was videotaped and I can watch it over and over again. I've had other memorable nights, but I forgot to tape them, so who cares?

Here's how my chance to guest-host *The Tonight Show*

presented itself. I had just gotten home from somewhere —who gives a shit—when I found a message on my answering machine from my agent, Leo. It said to call Johnny Carson's producer, Fred de Cordova. It seems Burt Reynolds was scheduled to guest-host *The Tonight Show* that week but had suddenly canceled because he had gotten angry and hit himself in the eye with his fist. De Cordova wanted to know if I'd be interested in taking Burt's place. I like Burt, and I'd hire him to be my bodyguard in a second.

"We want you to guest-host *The Tonight Show*," Fred said, "because you have that spontaneous wit and *some* of the audience likes you." Fred has his own brand of wit, and I admire him greatly. I couldn't find the exact words to thank him, so I said nothing.

I've never said this publicly, but Fred de Cordova reminds me of Artie, the man who became my own producer. Fred is a brilliant man who's been in show business for some time. I love him. He taught me a lot and prepared me to go on to do my own show. The best advice he ever gave me was, "Be yourself, if you know who the fuck that is."

De Cordova asked if this meant that my agent, Leo, would stop calling him three times a day. "Sure," I said. "It's worth having you host just for that!" Fred said.

Heeere's
Larry Sanders!

ELEVEN-THIRTY. NBC. THAT FIRST time I guest-hosted *The Tonight Show* my guests were Richard Dreyfuss, David Brenner, and Tom Cruise. It was a good show. Doc Severinsen sat in for Ed. Doc is a wonderful, charming, supportive man. I don't have one negative thing to say about him. On the other hand, his wife, Emily, picks out his clothes. What is she thinking? Doc's clothes, as Joyce Brothers whispered to me one day backstage, are a desperate cry for help.

The Severinsens have become like family to me, and I suppose that's why they never invite me to visit. I hear they spend all their time with nice guy Garry Shandling. I can tell Shandling thinks I'm shallow just from the intensity with which he says it to me.

I've always felt that Doc was a better foil for me than Ed because, frankly, he paid more attention. I would often see Ed counting the money in his wallet in the middle of one of Johnny's interviews. Doc, on the other hand, was alive and cherished the opportunity to sit on the couch. He didn't take it for granted. After the host's desk, I believe the couch is the second most sacred place on earth. The altar in the Vatican is third to both of these. Then comes Elle Macpherson's ass.

Today, Johnny Carson's whole *Tonight Show* set is in the Smithsonian Institution. I hear that when Letterman retires he wants his set turned into an amusement park. Jay's set is always different. I know that he switched from the ocean backdrop to a cityscape, which was an excellent move. It always looked like his set was on pontoons and that they were somehow shoved out into the water.

Jay confided to me, in fact, that many of his guests were getting seasick by midnight. During one commercial break Larry Hagman turned green and threw up on Matt LeBlanc. Jay insisted the set be changed and won a heated battle with the set designer, who insisted the solution was giving the guests Dramamine. "Get away from me before I kiss you," Jay warned him. The set was changed.

Whenever I visit Washington, D.C., the only two exhibits I regularly see are the old *Tonight Show* set and the Vietnam Veterans Memorial. They are both moving, but I think I saw more people die on *The Tonight Show*.

The Phone Call

A MONTH LATER I GUEST-HOSTED again. My guests that night were Herve Villechaize, may he rest in peace; Rock Hudson, may he rest in peace; Gary Busey, may he rest in peace; and a musical group that consisted of five young black men singing a cappella, I think. Who listens?

Later that night, at home, my phone rang.

"Hello, Larry?" a familiar voice said. "It's Johnny."

I said, "Yes, Johnny. I didn't mess up your desk. I didn't change your chair height. And I flushed the toilet, twice, I swear."

Johnny laughed. He said, "I just saw the show tonight."

I said, "Wow, I'm glad you watched. I'm honored. What did you think?"

"You were great," he said. "But remember you're there to make your guests look good. And don't forget to listen to your guests. Don't always be thinking about your next joke, because you're naturally funny. All you have to do is have a normal conversation."

I said, "Thanks for the advice. It means a lot to me." Then he said, "Also, about your makeup: it was too heavy, the eyebrow shading was too . . . You looked like a girl."

What Johnny said hurt me deeply. I've never really gotten over it. *He* wears makeup, why can't I? I guess everybody has a dark side, and I had just seen Johnny's. The way he lashed out about the makeup, the rage I sensed, surprised me, shocked me, and disappointed me. For God's sake, it's only makeup. Why did he have to go on and on about it? I suppose we'll never really know until Johnny writes a book. Which will probably never happen because the wounds are too deep. Makeup can't cover all the emotional scars. I know, I tried. I am not a girl.

It Was Bound
To Happen

BASED ON MY SUCCESS AS JOHNNY Carson's permanent guest-host—you can call the A. C. Neilsen company and they'll tell you that the ratings hardly dipped, and sometimes even stayed the same, the nights I sat in Johnny's chair—I was soon offered my own talk show ... opposite Johnny!

As luck would have it, I bumped into super-agent Michael Ovitz right as the offer came in. Ovitz was then ranked as the most powerful man in Hollywood by, I believe, *MAD* magazine. Mike hadn't yet quit the William Morris Agency to begin his own Creative Artists Agency, which would soon dominate the agency business. That day he was just at Long's Drugstore buying Mylanta by himself. Actually, he said that he needed it in such quantity that he was embarrassed to have his assistant shop for it any longer. He had two hundred bottles of it in his cart, but insisted some of them were gifts. I said, "Mike, may I get your advice?" I told him my predicament and he said, "Don't think twice about it. This is a no-brainer," which has now become a very popular phrase in Hollywood for describing a situation in which there is such a clear-cut choice that one doesn't even need to think about it. Up until then it meant Heather Thomas was on the phone. He said, "You jump. Start your own show because eventually there's going to be cable and interactive television and the Internet. The Japanese will buy Hollywood. The media is going to become so diverse you need to stake out your little piece of territory right now."

I said, "Mike, NBC and ABC are out of the question. But what do you think about CBS? My agent, Leo, thinks it's a bad idea."

Mike said, "He's right. Who in their right mind would want to go on CBS? It's a cemetery. It's the graveyard shift. I wouldn't advise anyone to go to CBS."

Ovitz seemed so sure of himself that I said, "Would you like to represent me in the deal?"

He said, "No."

I said, "Then I'm stuck with that putz Leo."

He said, "Sounds like it. I wouldn't want to be involved in this mess."

Years later he signed David Letterman and was intimately involved in getting Dave the four-billion-dollar contract that he now has with CBS. But I love Mike Ovitz. He's a good-hearted man who loves kids and charities as long as they don't cross him.

The Carson Feud

I THOUGHT I'D FEEL GREAT ABOUT THE chance to fulfill my lifelong dream, but I still felt very awkward taking the show because of Johnny. As you know from reading this far, one of my strongest attributes is my loyalty. It's one of the big messages I'm trying to get across in this book. So there I was, loyal to Johnny, and I would have remained loyal to Johnny except that they offered me my own show. I think that's the only possible reason not to remain loyal. I'm sure everyone would agree. If tomorrow someone offered you your own talk show, wouldn't you tell your current boss, "Good-bye, thanks for everything up to now"?

My big problem was that my new show was scheduled opposite *The Tonight Show.* If I accepted, Johnny Carson and I would be competing for viewers at 11:30 P.M.

My first instinct was to tell Johnny about the job offer. But I couldn't, because the syndicator and his publicity people insisted that it should be a surprise to everyone. If I told Johnny, word would get out before I'd signed the deal. Johnny would have to tell his producers. And the producers would, of course, tell the hookers, and that's how it would get back to the press. And then everyone would know, especially my needy, desperate relatives, who would be asking for cash or even worse: jobs. And my needy ex-partner who would also be looking for cash—or, as he called it, "bail." So I made the deal and promised to keep it secret. Then the company announced the deal before I could speak to Johnny. At least that's what I had to tell everyone.

I called up Johnny and said, "Johnny?" And he hung up on me. I was honored that he recognized my voice so quickly. And he was right to hang up on me.

I think Johnny Carson felt used by me. After all, he had been the major catalyst to my career for almost ten years, and now, suddenly, I was his competitor. I know I would be disappointed if someone did that to me.

When word of my new talk show hit the papers, along with the story about how I hadn't told Johnny first, there was a period in the press when they looked at me as some sort of opportunist. It's not the *worst* thing they could say about me. It was certainly better than getting a bad review. But the part about not being loyal really bothered me. It was totally false because I was loyal to Johnny for the year he allowed me to guest-host his show, until I got a better offer. I can't stress enough how everybody seems to conveniently forget that. You stay in a marriage until something better comes along. I'm kidding. You stay in a marriage until the other person has something better come along—at least that's been my experience.

PART FIVE

MY
OWN
SHOW

The First Night

EVEN THOUGH IT'S BEEN YEARS, I STILL RE-member the first night I hosted *The Larry Sanders Show* like it was yesterday. My side-kick Hank's gas pains were so bad that they rushed him to the hospital as he screamed, "Appendicitis! My God, my appendix is bursting." It was only later at the hospital after the x-ray that he remembered they had taken his appendix out when he was a teenager. Thank God you don't need an appendix to be a sidekick on a talk show. In fact, there's no medical proof that any organ is necessary.

The best-kept secret about opening night, and the single

event that, as far as I'm concerned, cemented my commitment to the job of TV talk show host, came ten minutes before airtime, when my first scheduled guest, Cybill Shepherd, walked into my dressing room to wish me luck. I wished her the same. She nervously began looking at me and then through a stack of telegrams on the coffee table. I picked one of them up and read it out loud:

"'Dear Larry, Who are you kidding? I'm the queen of late night! Signed, Joan Rivers.'"

We laughed. We laughed hard. Cybill loved Joan and predicted she would take me to the cleaners. The words came out of Cybill's mouth in a very sexy way. I grabbed her. Suddenly we were kissing. It happened that fast. She reached down between my legs and whispered seductively, "I just insulted you. Is that what you like?"

"Yes," I growled.

"Your balls are tiny," she gasped.

"Stop it, you're driving me crazy," I stammered.

Just then, Artie banged on the door. "Five minutes," he yelled. That's all the time I needed. One minute for the actual sex and four minutes to press my pants and fix my makeup.

But the sex was so good that we went the full five minutes, which meant I had to go on the air looking like shit.

But otherwise it was a perfect night for me because after sex, there's nothing I like to do more than go on stage and tell jokes to strangers.

Celebrity Sex

THE SHOW WAS A SEXUAL BUFFET FOR me. There were actresses and models and magician's assistants and beauty queens. And you name it. I once saw a picture of a beautiful blonde in *The New York Times* who had lost her house in a hurricane. The winds peaked at 120 miles an hour, and she nearly died. She had the most amazing body I'd ever seen.

"Let's book her," I said to Artie.

"Are you kidding? This story's a tragedy. Besides, you don't know if she'll look this good in person."

"Let's take a chance. That's what television is all about."

I was right. She was a knockout. The first ten minutes of the interview went badly because we had to get the hurricane shit out of the way. But once she revealed that she was single and loved to dance the lambada, I was home free. We dated for two weeks and when we broke up, she cried like it was another bad storm. I felt so bad I bought her a trailer. Ironically, two years later she was in *The New York Times*, standing next to a tattered cement foundation. The trailer was gone, taken by hurricane Hugo. We booked her again. She was on a total of six times over the years, but by hurricane Camille she had sort of let herself go and now I found her "bad luck" stories to be dull and not entertaining.

Around the same time I began using the date rape drug Rohypnol. I took it twenty times. I didn't know you were supposed to give it to the woman. The next morning I would wake up and ask, "Did I have sex with you?"

"No," I remember Carol Burnett saying once. "I would have, but you passed out."

"Dammit," I said. "I'm sorry."

"No, it's my fault," Carol said. "I went on and on with that Tim Conway story too long. I don't blame you for passing out. In fact, I was right behind you."

I feel awful telling tales out of school. So rather than go into private details that could be embarrassing, I'd rather just list all of the women that I have had sex with:

Cindy Crawford	Mariel Hemingway
Paula Abdul	a Mariah Carey look-alike
Mariah Carey	Helen Hunt
Shania Twain	Nancy Kerrigan
Cher	Diane Sawyer
Sinéad O'Connor	Margaret Cho
Julia Louis-Dreyfus	Dana Delany
Daphne Zuniga	Sharon Gless
Shelley Fabares	Uma Thurman
Uta Hagen	Rene Russo
Gwyneth Paltrow	Donna Rice
Anne Heche	Parker Posey
Christina Ricci	Gillian Anderson
both the Indigo Girls	Jennifer Lopez
Demi Moore	Drew Barrymore
Jamie Lee Curtis	Kim Basinger
Sigourney Weaver	Kirstie Alley
Frances McDormand	Jenna Elfman
Gretchen Mol	Andy Dick
Minnie Driver	Salma Hayek
Marisa Tomei	Daryl Hannah
Lesley Visser	Lea Thompson
Brooke Shields	the drummer for the Go-Go's
Carmen Electra	Connie Sellecca
Carrie Fisher	Audrey Hepburn
Noah Wyle's girlfriend	Grace Slick
Ellen DeGeneres	Julianna Margulies
Lorrie Morgan	Renee Zellweger

I was no longer the unloved fat boy that I was in high school.

Some of these women may deny having sex with me —as they did while they were doing it. I remember Courteney Cox yelling, "This isn't happening! This isn't happening!"

On second thought, that was me yelling that. My penis had hit some clear air turbulence. Courteney Cox wasn't even there.

My Daily Routine

BEING ON TV EVERY NIGHT IS HARD work. It requires enormous preparation. I wake up at about nine A.M. When I was married, I would pat the other side of the bed, first thing, to see if my wife was there. Usually she'd drift off during the evening and sleep in another room—at Harvey Keitel's house. I rise and go for about a two-mile run and then I have breakfast by myself. I try not to talk to anybody because it would use up my "conversational" energy. I find that if I'm silent the whole day, that by airtime I can't wait to say anything, which is really what's necessary to be a talk show host. Of course, it's equally important to be a good listener. So before the show I also don't listen to anyone. What no one knows—and I'm revealing it here for the first time—is that I wear earplugs all day long, and that is probably why some people think I have a "haughty" attitude. For instance, when a waitress comes to my table and I just point to something on the menu, then to my mouth, then to my ear, and then wave her away.

Oddly, Marlee Matlin, a frequent guest, has the exact opposite routine. Apparently, she prepares for an appearance on my show or any talk show by talking and listening all day long: You've got to do what you've got to do.

I have nine cups of coffee right before the show, within five minutes of actually walking on to do the monologue, to get charged up. I drink it absolutely black. Nine cups of black coffee. I don't think either cream or sugar is really healthy for you. One time I put a tablespoon of cocaine in my coffee and came shooting through the curtains before Hank had finished his introduction, and I had to make a recovery joke about Hank mistiming the intro because he was on Quaaludes.

I'm always very wired after the show. During the hour-long program, I have to push myself to a fever pitch in order to keep the guests and the audience entertained, because otherwise my normal energy level is that of Charlie Rose. But once that energy gets going and the audience responds, things tend to build on themselves, and before you know it your heart rate is up and you're feeling alive and charged, and really working at your peak. Occasionally you could see me put my fingers to my neck in order to check my pulse, because one time it reached 220 during a Robin Williams interview and I nearly had a stroke.

Suddenly, the show is over, I say "good-night," and everything comes to a deafening halt. I'm stuck with no one to talk to and no audience . . . just real life. Making that transition each night is painful and requires alcohol.

I go home to my empty house. I watch my own show every night and my heart rate jumps up again, but then the tape shuts off at 12:30, and I am stuck with an erection and want to have sex.

I remember once having Sandra Bullock over to my house after the show. We actually had a two-week fling. There was no sex, we just flung each other around. Sandra looked over at me and said, "Do you watch yourself every night?"

"Yes, all hosts do," I told her.

"Bill Maher doesn't," she said. "He watches pornography."

Always willing to better myself as a person, I stopped watching myself after my show and instead I would go over to Bill Maher's house. I was growing!

My Leadership

"IF YOU WANT SOMETHING DONE right, you have to do it yourself," O. J. Simpson once told me.

One night after Dana Carvey guest-hosted, I found my desk had been rearranged. Unbeknownst to me, my cigarette lighter ended up where my pencils were supposed to be. The paperweight had been moved to my coffee-cup spot. As I was interviewing Cindy Crawford during one of our special "live" shows, my mouth became dry and I reached for the cup. Instead, I ended up smashing my front two teeth with a big, heavy ceramic paperweight. Blood was dripping all over my notes. I stomped off.

"Who moved my stuff?" I yelled to the stage manager.

"I don't know," he said.

"Good answer."

Then I lost it. "I don't fucking care who fucking moved it. Just make sure it's in the same fucking place every fucking night." I sat back down at the desk and drank a cup of pencils. I was in the hospital for two days with lead poisoning. Nothing was ever out of place again. That's leadership.

Another night I discovered that someone had fiddled with the height adjustment of my chair. When I sat down I was an eighth of an inch lower than I had been the night before. Believe me, an eighth of an inch matters when you're a late night talk show host. Have you ever noticed that Dave's chair is two feet higher than the guest chair? My chair is only one and three-fourths inches higher than the guest chair because I'm not as insecure as Dave or Jay. Still, it was an eighth of an inch lower. "Who's been sitting in my chair ... ?" I started to lose control. "And who's been sleeping in my bed and eating my porridge?" The crew looked at me as if I were nuts, but I never saw so many wrenches pulled out so quickly. The chair was restored to its regular height and was never again out of place, except for when we lost George Burns. I lowered the chair to half-mast the day he died. That's my way of paying respect to those who are close to me.

The other time I really remember losing my temper was when my best friend, Jeff Goldblum, was on the show. Jeff and I are like brothers. I talk to him every day on the phone and I've seen everything he's done at least ten times. Some years ago, when he came on my show as a guest, I congratulated him for his performance in *The Crying Game*. He said, "I wasn't in *The Crying Game*." "Well, my notes say you were," I said. "Clearly there's some mistake. We'll be right back." During the commercial break, I stormed off. "Who the fuck did Jeff Goldblum's pre-interview, because he wasn't in the fucking *Crying Game*. He happens to be my best fucking friend. Do you know how embarrassing that is?"

Paula, who did the pre-interview, tried to convince me it was a typo. I sat back down at the desk and attempted a recovery. We were back on the air. "Jeff, before the commercial break, I mistakenly congratulated you for your performance in *The Crying Game*. That was a faux pas. What I meant, of course, was *The Onion Field*." Jeff said, "I wasn't in *The Onion Field*." "We'll be right back," I said. We took seventy-five commercial breaks that show and I never got one of his movies right, but we're still friends, because none of that stuff is important to me.

Team Sanders

THE STAR OF *THE LARRY SANDERS Show* is of course me, Larry Sanders. But it takes more than one person to make a talk show function at its best each night. Or as Hillary Rodham Clinton put it, "It takes a village." And by that I guess she meant no interns. We have 752 interns on *The Larry Sanders Show*. And it's none of your business what goes on between me and them, as long as I do my job each night. Why do we have this sick need-to-know obsession about people's personal lives? Moral character is important, but as Judge Wapner said, "Judge not, lest ye be judged." We are a self-destructing race. The troubles started with the Big Bang. Everything was fine up until then. No one wants to face the real truth: that life is impermanent and full of suffering. Sorry for this negative digression, but I forgot to take my medication today. Okay, I just did.

Now, let me tell you a little about the Sanders team:

Artie

A RTIE, MY PRODUCER, IS A TRUE show business legend. He's also a terrific producer.

Artie is from New York. He started as a bouncer at a strip club in the early 1950s and then produced a local radio talk show. Artie got his big break when he was asked to run *The Tonight Show* with Jack Paar. Paar, it seems, was a frequent guest on the radio show, and he and Artie would go out drinking afterward. This says something about the enduring power of show business connections, and even more about the bonding power of alcohol. Paar, as we all know, was a brilliant man who eventually walked off his show and made way for Johnny Carson's thirty-year reign. When Paar walked, Artie also walked. Actually, he was dragged.

Artie's next job was producing *The Jackie Gleason Show* out of Miami Beach. Artie and Jackie had a big fight one day when Artie told Jackie that his famous "And away we go" catch phrase should be changed to "Away I go." They argued well through the night and into the spring. It was resolved when Artie finally said, "Well, away I go, because I quit."

After I signed to do *The Larry Sanders Show* the network said to me, "Who do you see producing your show?" They had hired me and then I had to put the whole package of people together for them to approve. I said I'd like someone young and hip. They said, "What about Arthur?"

I said, "You mean the legendary Artie . . . ?"

They said, "Yeah."

"Well, don't you think he's passé?" I asked. "I mean, I know that he's legendary and all, but . . ."

"Why don't you just have a meeting with him?" they suggested.

I called Artie and we arranged to have lunch at Le Dome, a high-priced showbiz hangout on Sunset Boulevard.

As soon as we sat down to lunch in the glass-enclosed patio, the legendary Artie ordered a Salty Dog (half salt, half dog) and said to me, "A talk show is about the host.

The ratings will vary with the notoriety of the guests, but on a nightly basis over the long haul the audience tunes in to see the host."

I said, "Would you like another Salty Dog?"

He said, "Yes, thank you." Then he said, "But the host's job is to make the guests look good. And by making the guests look good, the host automatically looks good."

Artie knew everything there was to know about talk shows. And though he wasn't the youngest guy with the newest ideas, he was a wise man who seemed to sense the core of what talk shows were about. I said, "I would like you to produce my talk show."

He said, "Fuck you. I'm just here for the free lunch."

That clinched it. I said, "Would you like another Salty Dog?"

"No," he said, "I got the job." With that, he stood up and left. Our relationship since has been more than producer-star, it's been father-daughter, particularly in the sense that after a bad show he'd spank me. He stopped doing that shortly after the Menendez trial.

Hank

HANK KINGSLEY IS MY TRUSTY SIDE-kick. I met him on a cruise ship, where he was the cruise director. I was on vacation.

Hank would announce the activities of the day to the passengers each morning at eight A.M. I was fortunate enough to hear him each day without fail because my room was right above where he stood on the main deck. The first time we spoke I opened my porthole and shouted, "Hey, I'm trying to sleep! Shove that megaphone up your ass!" He yelled back, "That's one of the planned activities for later!" The guests gathered around him on the deck laughed and looked up and yelled, "Hey, it's Larry Sanders!"

Hank was just a talk show host's sidekick waiting to happen. In fact he referred to himself as the "Captain's Sidekick" on the cruise and insisted the boat couldn't function without him.

The next day, as luck would have it, I met Hank as he was trying to rip the life jacket off a young boy during the first safety drill. He was yelling, "Hey now! Gimme that life jacket, you little bastard! Me first." He had forgotten that it was a drill and panicked. I pulled his hands away from the young boy and said to Hank, "I believe it's just a drill."

He said, "Really? I'm so hung over I can't tell the bells and the whistles from the sirens and screams I hear in my head."

"No," I said, "this is a drill." Then I said I'd just been offered a late night talk show on the network and I was looking for a sidekick. Someone who would be there every night, someone I could make fun of, to make me look funnier.

"You mean a co-host?"

I said, "No, a sidekick."

"You mean a partner?" he said.

"No, I mean a sidekick," I said.

"You mean like a lifetime soulmate?"

I said, "No. Like a fucking sidekick who sits on the couch and laughs at everything I say."

"Oh," he said, "I'd love to."

Just then the boat capsized, throwing Hank into the water without a life jacket. I was wrong. It was not a drill.

Beverly

PERHAPS THE MOST IMPORTANT PERSON in my life is my assistant, Beverly. I don't really know anything about her. She's been with me twelve years and I just recently discovered that she's black.

She's intelligent, funny, and a real caretaker. Her instincts are impeccable, and I have often relied on her to tell me which monologue jokes were funny before the show. I love her dearly, and now that the show is over I hope to get to know her better. I'm in the process of trying to find her to see what she's currently doing and to see if she knows where my favorite plaid socks disappeared to.

Stevie Grant

STEVIE GRANT, MY EX-AGENT, IS a good guy, smart and talented, but he became so scared by success that he didn't know how to handle it and lost himself. Arrogance is overcompensation for insecurity. Who would know that better than a performer? I'm not saying that's true of me, but it is for every other performer I know. The more frightened Stevie got, the more arrogant he became and the more he came to believe that success was just about perception and image. "Honesty should be left to those creative nuts," he said to his real mother.

"I don't know who you are anymore," his mom replied.

"No one does. That's the beauty of it, Mom!"

He moved further from the truth and became more controlling. In the last few years he began using intimidation tactics. "Don't fuck with me," he would tell everyone from clients to network executives. "It's a small town—I'll make it very difficult for you." It's when I heard him say it to his dog that I knew it was mostly hot air, although his dog has had trouble getting work lately.

What Stevie really wanted was to be in the Mafia, or, at the very least, one of the *Godfather* movies. He just didn't have the balls for one or the connections for the other. So he pretended. On Halloween, as late as last year, he would dress up as Al Capone and go door-to-door in his neighborhood. Instead of asking for candy, he would tell the kindly homeowners that they had to start paying him one hundred dollars a month protection money, or else. To convince them that he wasn't kidding, he would yank his mask off and yell, "Does it look like I'm kidding?" He actually pulled in an extra grand a month through this scam. When he finally moved to a bigger home on the other side of town, the old neighbors had a block party that lasted a week.

Last year, Stevie finally went to get some therapy. "I'd like to understand myself better," he told me, but he told the shrink that any details about his personal life and behavior were on a "need-to-know basis." That led nowhere, and instead he chose to go to physical therapy, where he sat in a whirlpool tub for fifty minutes. "I'm really getting to know myself!" he shouted to the man sitting in the tub next to him.

He was softening up. Just a few weeks after he started therapy, he said to me, "A Jackie Chan is more than a client, he's like a brother who's a client." Then he added, "This therapy's been good for me. My lower back has never been better."

I recently received a letter from Stevie, postmarked Oslo. "Larry, I've moved here to Sweden or wherever the fuck Oslo is. If you're ever in Scandinavia, call me. I started a small production company with Lasse Hallström, the director. By the way, I was looking at an old photo of us, and I believe that I now use more lip gloss than you."

I don't know what the hell that last part meant, but it's hard to imagine it's true.

I miss him.

Critics

I LOVE ALL CRITICS AND BOOK REVIEW-
ers. Although why did Tom Shales have to
say the band was bad? The more you draw
attention to it, the worse they feel. It's just
not fair. They did the best they could with
the drugs they had.

The Guests

A TALK SHOW IS NOTHING WITHOUT good guests. And I've been lucky to have a lot of them. I've always thought a picture is worth a thousand words—especially for those people who can't read. So here's a little something for people who can read: pictures and words.

LARRY SANDERS

DAVID DUCHOVNY

David Duchovny has been on the show more than any other handsome male guest. Here he is in 1995 taking a cheap shot at the size of my ass. He is explaining that in the makeup room he saw me begging Cindy Crawford for some of her "contour makeup" to make my ass look thinner.

Cindy responded by saying, "There isn't enough makeup in my bag to cover your ass. And besides, aren't you going to be wearing pants tonight?" "Never mind," I said. "You models just like to keep all of the beauty and makeup secrets for yourselves." And I walked out . . . backward.

DAVID LETTERMAN

Here I am in 1992, after presenting Dave Letterman with either the American Television Award or a lit cigar. I don't remember which it was, but he couldn't have been more removed and cordial. I am a big fan, and he was nice enough to call me after my final show to say, "It's about time."

JENNIE GARTH

Here is a photo of Jennie Garth from Beverly Hills 90210.
I had sex with her a dozen times, but she never reciprocated.
Her excuse was, "I like men." She is beautiful and talented,
and if by some fluke I ever do a talk show again I hope that
she will be my third guest.

SHARON STONE

As you can see, I can't take my eyes off the necklace I had given Sharon the night before the show. Those are real diamonds, and it cost me two-and-a-half million dollars. By the way, the tie that I am wearing is also real and was given to me by . . . the wardrobe person. Sharon's never given me anything, but it's the thought that counts.

HAPPY LARRY

People say they hardly ever see me smiling. Here is a photo that was taken of me with a hidden camera. I had been smiling like this the entire day, hoping that a picture might be taken.

ED BEGLEY

Ed Begley rides his bike everywhere. Here he is trying to apologize to me for chaining it to my leg.

PAT SAJAK

Pat Sajak was always angry that he didn't get the big guests when he was the guest host. Here he is interviewing a man from the audience. What is he complaining about?

ED MCMAHON

Ed McMahon is a terrific dancer. I can't imagine Fred Astaire being any lighter on his feet. This photo was taken at my home during a party at which there was only myself, Ed, and the photographer.

HANK'S WEDDING

Hank wanted to be married on the show, à la Tiny Tim,
Hank's idol. The marriage only lasted a year, and he
wanted to have the divorce on the air as well, but Artie and
I felt that divorce was too much reality for a late night television audience. Hank was angry and sold the rights to his
divorce to the Weather Channel, which covered it only from
their satellite camera. "We looked like fucking ants!" Hank
said to me one day when I was trying not to listen.

ALEC BALDWIN

Hank always wanted to be one of the Baldwin brothers, but Artie, who was in a foul mood because he had just passed a kidney stone from the back, said, "The closest you will ever get to being a Baldwin brother is the Bald part." Even I winced and said, "Excuse me, I have to make a phone call."

DANA DELANY

The tabloids had a field day with a story that Dana Delany was not interested in me and that we never went out. To the contrary, she begged for sex often from me, and we had it over and over for a total of two times. I filed a suit against the tabloid for circulating such a false story and for demeaning my character by implying that Dana Delany was not interested in me. I would have won millions of dollars in this suit had Dana Delany not testified that she in fact was not interested in me. The system sucks.

BRUNO KIRBY *and* STEVEN WRIGHT

Two of my best friends are Bruno Kirby and Steven Wright. We hang out together all the time. They both happened to be on the show together in 1994. It was one of the worst shows we ever did. I don't know why.

My relationship with Bruno later became strained because he was bumped every time he was scheduled to appear. "Why do you even bother to book me?" he screamed at me during one of our couples therapy sessions. I said, "Hey, who's paying for this?"

SUZANNE SOMERS

Suzanne Somers is a wonderful guest and a sweetheart. Her famous Thighmaster, which sold for only $39.00, is still one of the best dates I have ever had.

BRIDGET FONDA

Sparks really flew the night Bridget Fonda was on.
The entire underside of my desk was charred beyond
recognition. Artie said, "The fire marshals told me that
we can't have her on again. It's just too dangerous."

DUCHOVNY AGAIN

Here is another time that David Duchovny took a cheap shot at the size of my ass. He seemed to find nothing funnier. "You are really well hung from the back," he said. The audience howled, and I just looked down to my notes for my next question.

THE DUCHOVNY
REPRIMAND

This picture was taken of Duchovny during a commercial break when Artie came over to warn Duchovny to stop taking such cheap shots at my ass.

LAURA LEIGHTON

I heard that Laura Leighton has recently gotten married. I am heartbroken. We dated off and on, or as Laura referred to it, "off." I would marry her tomorrow if she would let me know by seven P.M. so I could change my schedule.

ELLEN DEGENERES

I am proud to say that I slept with Ellen DeGeneres long before Anne Heche did. Let's just leave it at that.

STING

I had bumped into Sting at the water cooler where he told me, "I am only doing your show to plug my new album."

"I know that," I said. He was fantastic on the show that night. A real artist. I wish he could have done a whole song, but we were running short.

RICHARD BELZER

Richard Belzer is a very funny comedian in addition to being a very fine actor on the series Homicide. *He also happens to have a great outside basketball shot, but unfortunately we play inside.*

JERRY SEINFELD

Jerry Seinfeld is the richest friend I've got. It always makes him feel awkward when I say that to his face, because he knows it really comes from my heart.

HOWARD STERN

Howard once told me, "You know you're gay if you're hav-
ing sex with a man, but fantasizing it's another man." I told
him, "You know you're gay when you bend over and see
four balls." We went on like that all night. I actually know
nothing about the man himself.

HUGH HEFNER

*Hugh Hefner is the one on the left. I had him on so I could
meet girls. He introduced me to Miss October, whom
I almost had sex with, but she used the flimsy excuse that
it was November and I had missed her by only a couple of
days. "What do I look like, an idiot?" she asked.*

TOM SNYDER

Tom Snyder never stopped looking at the camera like this throughout the entire interview. I never once saw him from the front. What a master!

BOB COSTAS
and JIM GRAY

Bob Costas and Jim Gray think that they know everything about sports. Big deal. I'm more macho than them and their wives put together.

JENNIFER ANISTON

Jennifer Aniston is one of the most beautiful women that we have ever had on the show aside from Warren Beatty. It is true that all of the Friends go everywhere together. All of the others were sitting backstage waiting for her to finish her segment on my show. I asked her in a commercial break if I could be one of the Friends, and she said, "Not even a Pen Pal." Jennifer is a hypochondriac. I remember the first time she appeared on the show. She said, "No, I will not tongue-kiss you." I said, "I swear, I don't have a cold or anything," but I guess she's just too "germ crazy."

LARRY SANDERS
HOST

ADAM SANDLER

Adam Sandler is one of the funniest comedians we ever had on the show. I particularly enjoyed his song parodies and the respect he shows me. I think Adam really looks up to me as a mentor and that's what makes him so special. He's a big fan of mine, and I enjoy giving him advice about his career and the way he dresses. Sometimes I feel like a big sister to him. He has a big movie career now and invites me to all the premieres. He picks me up in his own car and never charges me for gas. He is a nice Jewish boy except for the fact that I think he gets laid a lot. He has told me that he believes that Hank gets in his way on the show, even when Hank is away on vacation. "Knowing that he might even be watching makes me sick," Adam says.

BEN STILLER

Here is a photo of Ben Stiller explaining to me how sexy he thinks he is. As you can see, Hank is fascinated, because he agrees. By the time this book comes out, I predict Ben will be a giant movie star. We sometimes play basketball together and he is a sensational athlete when he is not stopping to describe how sexy he is. I guess he's sexy—if you're a girl! Where does that get you?

We have also had his parents, Anne Meara and Jerry Stiller, on the show. During a commercial break once, they told me that Ben was adopted and they wished that Adam Arkin was their son instead.

CHRIS ELLIOTT

Chris Elliott will do anything, including my show. That is a lovable quality, according to Ed Begley. Chris makes me laugh and laugh until I'm hard. I mean, laugh hard.

KEVIN NEALON

Comedian Kevin Nealon is a favorite guest but difficult to book because he's represented by the William Morris Agency, ICM, CAA, UTA, and Endeavor. He says, "If an agent can have a hundred clients, why can't a client have a hundred agents?"

JEFF GOLDBLUM

Jeff Goldblum is the most suave man I know. He's also an extraordinarily talented actor, a gifted musician, and built like a Gentile. Here he is fixing his tie while he's playing the piano. What a master!

LARRY ALONE AT THE DESK

Sometimes I just stare at this picture and miss myself.

CLINT BLACK

*Clint Black is a good friend of mine. People don't know that
I love country music, and in fact when I was a boy I
dreamed of being a rodeo clown. A witty rodeo clown.
I would come out of the barrel and say to the bull,
"I've seen better horns on a Volkswagen."*

THE MERMAID SKETCH

I love doing sketch work. I've done over two million sketches on the show. My favorite character of course is Big Roscoe, the porno star, and Wing Lu, the gay Chinese weatherman. I only played Jimmy the Horny Sailor once, because we received so many letters from sailors saying no sailor is named Jimmy.

I like doing sketch work because it allows me to stretch as an actor. Although I don't know what that means. But I enjoy making jokes and getting laughs and receiving pay. Therefore I enjoy sketch work.

NORM MACDONALD

Norm MacDonald is one of those comedians who can't stop talking about his penis off the air. "My penis needs a ride home. My penis is hungry. My penis is sad and lonely. My penis needs makeup. Hank won't let go of my penis. Don Ohlmeyer's penis fired my penis." Et cetera . . . We had his penis on the show a dozen times and it was always a delight.

REGIS PHILBIN

*It's always difficult for one host to interview another host. The
interview goes like this:*

"Regis, how are you today?" I begin.

"How are you today, Larry?" Regis responds.

"How's your show coming along?" I answer.

"How's yours?" Regis queries.

"Shall we take a commercial break?" I ask.

"We'll be right back," Regis responds.

*In the commercial break Regis says, "Want to trade
Hank for Kathie Lee?"*

HELEN HUNT

Here I am telling Helen Hunt that I believed she would one day win an Academy Award. "Stop it, you're killing me," she said. "I can't breathe." One time I made Kelsey Grammer laugh so hard on the show that he peed in my pants.

HANK *and*

This was our regular Lotto sketch. Hank hoped that doing this sketch would result in his being offered the job as the announcer for the real lottery here in California, and it did. He was fired the first day because instead of calling the actual numbers that came up, he

THE LOTTERY

instead called the numbers on his ticket that he had bought the day before.

"You can't blame a guy for trying," Hank told the federal officials as they dragged him out of the studio.

DANA CARVEY

Dana Carvey does a wicked impression of me. They say that imitation is the highest form of flattery, but his impression is exaggerated and mean-spirited. Every other impression he does is on the mark and hilarious, especially his Jay Leno impression, where he straps on a large chin and talks in a high, whiny voice. That one cracks me up.

ILLEANA DOUGLAS

See pages 225–227 for how I blew this one.

LARRY and **THE CHIMP**

This was one fickle chimp. One appearance she'd be kissing me; the next she'd be grabbing my crotch. It was the same way whenever Heather Locklear was on the show.

TIM CONWAY

I never laughed harder than when Tim was on the show, but he always stole every shrimp in the Green Room. He never got caught, because a security guard never had the nerve to say, "Mr. Conway, what's that fishy smell coming from your pants?" It was the perfect crime and he knew it. I am certain that he's been ripping off seafood restaurants for years.

SUGAR RAY LEONARD

*I once boxed a round in a sketch we did with Sugar Ray
Leonard, I think. I don't remember. He hit me so hard
I didn't wake up until we were in court.*

PIE-EATING SKETCH

This is the famous pie-eating sketch that we ran on almost every anniversary show because Hank ate so quickly that he actually threw up on the air, the kind of talk show moment that you pray for.

BERNADETTE PETERS

Bernadette Peters referred to me as her Mandy Patinkin.
Mandy Patinkin referred to me as his Bernadette Peters.
It was incredibly awkward when the three of us would get
together because I never knew which part of the song
I should sing.

LARRY SANDERS
HOST

LARRY ALONE #2

Sometimes I stare at this picture and miss myself . . . sexually.

JOHN STAMOS

John Stamos thinks that he is the most handsome man alive. You take a look and be the judge. I'll take myself any day of the week, mainly because I have.

HANK

Hank was always there for me. He would laugh at monologue jokes he didn't even get. I loved him for that. He's a good man and I will miss him because now that the show is over I don't intend to ever see him again. I'm just kidding. In fact, we went out for dinner just the other night and he begged me to start up another talk show because he was really having trouble getting work. By six A.M. we were lying drunk in a whorehouse in south central Los Angeles.

"This is like old times, isn't it?" Hank sighed.

I Was Feeling
Special Again

I N 1991 I GOT MY SECOND PEOPLE'S
Choice Award in a row as Favorite Television Personality. Liza Minnelli presented it
to me in an emotional moment. We had slept
together once or twice in the late seventies,
and when I broke it off, she was crushed. I
had avoided Liza after that, and she had
drifted from one bad relationship to
another. I always knew, and would hear it
from friends, that she'd never gotten
over me, and that night, through the
magic of television, the whole world
could see the tears in Liza's eyes
when we finally saw each other

again and she handed me the statuette. I'll never forget what she said next.

"The only regret I have in my life is that I ever let you touch me."

"You look beautiful tonight," I said, thinking there might be a chance we could get together after the show. I had tears in my eyes, too, but only because I had gotten a standing ovation. There's nothing like getting that kind of love from your peers. For me to look down and see Dave Letterman and Jay Leno and Richard Simmons all standing there looking up at me meant everything to me. I felt very, very special. In fact, in my speech, I said, "There was a very awkward time when I was fifteen that I will not go into now, but I was left very devastated by the fact that I no longer felt special, and you've made up for that. I want to thank you." The speech was later reprinted in the monthly SAG-AFTRA newsletter, and I heard that Sally Field cut it out and pinned it to her bedroom wall.

That was also my last People's Choice Award. I haven't even been nominated since 1991, even though I once co-hosted the show with Dean Cain and Rita Moreno. But that doesn't surprise me, because the audience is fickle and those awards mean nothing. If there's one thing I've learned, it's that you can't place any importance on anything but the work itself. So-called rewards are meaningless.

Well, that's not completely true.

When I was thirteen and a high school freshman, I

had a crush on my teacher. Her name was Mrs. Bernhardt, and she was beautiful. She was probably thirty-five. An older woman.

Twenty years later, at my high school reunion, Mrs. Bernhardt was one of the teachers who came back to see the class. She was still very attractive. To me, her white hair made her even hotter. I made a beeline for her.

After we'd danced, I told her it would mean a lot to me if we could go back to the schoolroom where we'd met.

We slipped out of the hotel and drove to old Washbash High, which was only a few minutes away. In the car, she asked how my life was going. She said she had enjoyed seeing me become successful on TV. At that time, I'd been doing my current show for only a year or two. I remember I kept sliding closer to her on the bench seat of her old Plymouth station wagon, which was no easy task because I was driving.

"Why are we driving to the other end of the school?"

I didn't want to tell her it was the beginning of my fantasy. So I told her that I was still lazy, but I was working on it all the time.

I couldn't keep my secret from her very long. We'd only been in the schoolroom a few moments when I told her about how I'd once had the biggest crush on her. Before I knew it, she was kissing me. Bobby pins were flying out of her hair like a bad science fiction movie. When I finally managed to push her away I said, "Isn't it ironic? Here I am almost fulfilling a fantasy of mine."

"And what would that fantasy be?" she said.

I raised my hand and she called on me. I whispered into her ear and she said, "Let's do it." I said okay. I couldn't believe it was really happening. I swear to you, she took off her clothes and, completely naked, picked up that long, wooden pointer and went up to the map holder in the front of the room. She bent over and pulled down a map of Civil War America—what a tease!

As we were humping, I realized we were doing it on my original desk. The desk she had nearly failed me on. I don't think she'd fail me now.

When we were done, she looked at me and said, "D-minus." I was ecstatic. I knew I could improve on my "F."

Then she said, "I have always wanted to have sex with a talk show host."

That's when I became aware of the power of my profession. I also remembered that Greg Kinnear, who was the host of *Later*, was scheduled to perform in Minneapolis that weekend and realized I was fortunate to have gotten to Mrs. Bernhardt first.

Burnout

I HAD BEEN HOSTING THE SHOW FOR ten years and had done over 10,000 interviews, two of which were good. Not one of the guests ever asked, "What projects have you got coming up, Larry?" It was always about them. How many times did I hear Harrison Ford say, "My next movie is in Africa, Larry"? What he was thinking was, "My life is exciting. I get to travel, meet new people, and kiss famous actresses while you're stuck behind that desk every night. Have fun with David Copperfield. I'm sure he'll be hilarious." Then David Copperfield would come on and plug his European tour or his next sexual encounter with Claudia Schiffer, which are the same thing. He told me that when he gets an erection he passes a hoop over it to show there are no wires attached. One time after he made an appearance on the show, my wallet was missing. I know Copperfield was responsible. He probably grabbed it while I was hitting on one of his beautiful magician's assistants, Bianca. That's what they are there for—it's called a diversion. What a gimmick. You stare at them while Copperfield cleans out your office. Ninety-five percent of all magicians are kleptomaniacs who have gone off the deep end. That's why they take such pleasure in making objects disappear. To them, it's just stealing. Mark my words: One day David Copperfield goes into a bank with two of his babes and cleans out the vault, if he hasn't done it already.

Everyone I interviewed seemed to have an interesting and dynamic career and life. I would read Lisa Kudrow's pre-interview and I remember feeling like a shut-in. She and her husband had just come back from a vacation in Italy, and she had a very funny story about paying $100 for a ravioli. On the air I said, "For that price, it must have been stuffed with one hundred dollars." Big laugh, but so what? She had the happy life. She had all the Friends from her show and she was making a movie. "Larry Sanders is just a pit stop on the way to everything else" is the way she put it to me backstage.

I began to feel used. I began to feel like one of my ex-wives. Celebrities were only coming on the show to plug a product. I, on the other hand, actually enjoyed talking to celebrities without any hidden agenda. Oh sure, I'd rather have Madonna on the show than the lady from *Touched by an Angel*, but mainly because we'd get better ratings. Otherwise, I would just as much enjoy talking to what's-her-name.

I tried to become friends with, let's say, a Michael Douglas. But those guys are movie stars with private planes and I'm just a man behind a desk. In fact, as Artie always put it, I'm "half-man, half-desk." Hank, Artie said, is one-fourth couch and three-fourths man.

It was time to quit the show. I was not having fun and I was not happy. Not that I ever thought those two went hand-in-hand. Besides, my ratings were slipping. I told the network executives that I was going to leave the show when my contract ended. "Good," they said. But nothing they could do would talk me out of it. My mind was made up, and when I said good-bye to the audience on that final night, I knew I was doing the right thing.

The Morning After

I AWOKE THE MORNING AFTER MY LAST TV show (May 30, 1998) feeling basically the same as I had for the last ten years, except for one thing: I felt different. It was less a feeling than a psychological problem. Who was I? What would I do?

I had a date with Illeana Douglas that afternoon. We had always gotten along well, but I had been consumed with my show and knew that my life was out of balance and that it was affecting our relationship. I promised her I would make up for lost time once the show ended, and Illeana was very patient with me. She waited until my final good-bye was said to the TV audience, and then, as I was walking off the stage, she ran up to me and yelled, "We have a date tomorrow at two at the Los Angeles Zoo. You owe me." She was right, I owed her $150 that I had borrowed for dinner one night because I had left my credit cards in my wallet, which was tucked away in the back pocket of the suit that I was wearing. Illeana Douglas is beautiful, sensitive, and highly intelligent, not to mention sexy—but I just did. I was a new man, completely committed to this relationship with nothing standing in my way now. I was three hours late for our first date. I arrived at the zoo on time, but then I began signing autographs out front and telling stories and the time began to zip by. I guess I signed only three or four autographs, but my stories went on and on. I could tell that the security guard and the little lost boy were getting bored, which is when I realized, "My God, I don't know how to act offstage. I'm a talk show host out of my natural environment." I glanced across the zoo at the polar bear standing in what must have been eighty-degree water and knew just what he must be feeling. I was no longer Larry Sanders the TV star, I was a man people no longer needed to help their friends get a job or give their clients a break or get them free tickets ... My celebrity powers were disappearing, and I felt very naked to the world. I don't mind *being* naked but I don't like *feeling* naked. I no longer get my favorite table at the restaurant even though I own it.

Fame and money bring nothing but money and fame. Who am I? What will I do?

I found Illeana feeding the llamas by hand. "How long have you been waiting?" I asked. "Three hours," she said. "Look at my fingers. They've been eaten down to the first joint." Llamas don't know when to stop. I rushed her to the hospital, but it was too late. We broke up in the car.

What's Next?

NOW THAT I CAN'T JUST CALL UP PEOPLE to put them on the show, I am trying to figure out a new way to meet people and make friends. I almost opened up a candle shop in West Hollywood, but it was smack in the middle of the gay section and I felt uneasy. Too bad, because the shop I wanted to buy was sooo adorable and sooo quaint. I could picture just how I wanted to fix it up and what I would wear, and I love candles, especially the sweetly scented ones. If only the shop hadn't been in West Hollywood. By the way, I'm still surprised by who turns up gay in show business. I will never forget my shock at walking into the men's room backstage at the show to discover the Smothers Brothers making out.

I decided to go "online," where there would be plenty of new people for me to meet. And was I right. The first night I checked into a chat room someone wanted to blow me, someone wanted to kill me, and someone wanted to talk to the person who wanted to blow me. It reminded me too much of my show, and I just yanked out the power cord.

Hours after the show ended, I bought a house in Malibu right next to Johnny Carson's. I spend the days sitting out on the beach and walking back and forth across Johnny's property, hoping to bump into him so we can talk about our talk show experiences, but so far I haven't seen him. His friends insist he has a phone, but I haven't been able to get the number from anyone. I'm sure it's his attempt to respect my privacy. He knows what it's like to come down from the kind of whirlwind success we talk show hosts experience, and I appreciate his consideration. But enough is enough. If Johnny reads this I hope he will feel comfortable enough to come by and say, "Hi, Larry, I'm a big fan and miss watching you every night."

Johnny, I leave the door unlocked on Tuesday nights, so just come in and sit down, because I would love to compare notes with you about . . . everything! Or even better, let's go to Disneyland sometime with the Rickleses and the Newharts.

My Last Interview

THERE IS ONLY ONE INTERVIEW THAT I've never done—that I hope to do—that I look forward to doing. My interview with God. There is really no bigger guest. And I'm sure it will be tough, because I know that God will want to be in control of the interview, much like Warren Beatty, who let's just say was never an interview I looked forward to. Beatty hides behind that handsome face and hopes you lose yourself in his eyes while he says absolutely nothing about anything. But he's not fooling me: He's gay. If I'm wrong, may God forgive me.

Upon my death—which will

be a sad day for show business and the entire Muslim world
—I imagine my interview with God would go something
like the following, assuming that I had decent pre-interview notes.

(*From his regular talk show desk.*)

<u>Larry</u>
My next guest needs no introduction.
Ladies and gentlemen, God.
(*God saunters on to a literally thunderous ovation.*)

<u>Larry</u>
God, so good to see you.

<u>God</u>
Happy to be here, Larry. You look great.
Been on vacation?

<u>Larry</u>
Hey, I'll ask the questions, but thank you, yes I have.
I was having a nice swim in the Pacific off Waikiki
when I suddenly took a speedboat in the head . . . but
let's stick with you. Do you do any impressions?

<u>God</u>
Yes, I do.

<u>Larry</u>
Really. Like . . .

<u>God</u>
Like anyone. Because, I am everyone.

Larry
Do Bogart.

God
From *The African Queen* or perhaps
Casablanca? Which, frankly, I'm
tired of—

Larry
Casablanca.

God
Ilsa, I'm no good at being noble, but it doesn't
take much to see that the problems of three
little people don't amount to a hill of beans in this
crazy world. Someday you'll understand that. . . .
Here's looking at you, kid.

Larry
That is unbelievable! It's like it's actually
him.

God
It is.

Larry
Right . . . I see . . . By the way,
do I get any points for being famous?

God
No.

Larry
Any points for the money?

God

No.

Larry

The pussy?

God

No. And you should be thankful I have a sense of
humor, because "pussy" is a demeaning word that
should only be used to mean "sissy."

Larry

I'll remember that.

God

No need to. You're not going back.

Larry

Where am I going?

God

Ah, that's the question. Where do you want to go?

Larry

I don't know.

God

Yes, that's the problem.

Larry

I see . . . I've just been flailing around
like an asshole, haven't I?

God

Yes.

<u>Larry</u>

"Asshole" doesn't bother you?

<u>God</u>

No, just "pussy."

<u>Larry</u>

So, instead of flailing around trying to—

<u>God</u>

Become famous.

<u>Larry</u>

Right?

<u>God</u>

And rich and everything else . . .

<u>Larry</u>

I should have spent more time . . .

<u>God</u>

. . . Trying to figure out what you were *without*
those things. That's what's important.

<u>Larry</u>

Well, I guess I could start right now
because I have no show or money
or pus— Sorry.

<u>God</u>

You've got the time now. By the way, Larry,
I loved you more when you were the fat boy
in school.

Larry
Really?

God
Yes.

Larry
(*Speechless for a moment.*)
Well, you've been a terrific guest.
Can you stay for Bob Hope?

God
Yes, I can. I'd love to.
He should be here any minute.

Larry
Good. We'll be right back with God
after this break—

God
I've always wanted to say this part: "No flipping."

Just my luck, my best interview and no one will have seen it. If only I could have booked him while I was alive, but then the truth of the matter is Artie would have bumped him for Jewel.

I've Got
the Time Now

Tahiti, 1998

L IFE IS SHORT. I AM LUCKY ENOUGH TO HAVE
the time to reflect upon it. I am happy and content, and
have lost two pounds just in my ass.

I love you all. I'll be back.

ABOUT THE AUTHOR

Not to be too metaphysical, but I, Larry Sanders, am a fictional character. I do not exist. No one does. We are all energy, especially Don Rickles. None of the things in this book really happened, and besides, my memory is so bad I don't believe the dates or the people are accurate. In other words: It's fiction.

I want to thank Kelly Grant, Dominick Anfuso, and Gordon McKee for their help.